ULYSSES S. GRANT

ULYSSES S. GRANT

KATE HAVELIN

LERNER PUBLICATIONS COMPANY/MINNEAPOLIS

This book is for my father, Dudley W. Havelin, who loved reading war history, and to my husband, Leo Timmons, and son, William Havelin, to whom the Civil War is as real as any other part of our lives.

Lerner Publications Company
A division of Lerner Publishing Group
241 First Avenue North
Minneapolis, MN 55401 U.S.A.

Website address: www.lernerbooks.com

Library of Congress Cataloging-in-Publication Data

Havelin, Kate, 1961–
    Ulysses S. Grant / by Kate Havelin.
       p.   cm. — (Presidential leaders)
    Summary: A biography of the commander of the Union forces in the Civil War who became the eighteenth president of the United States.
    Includes bibliographical references and index.
    ISBN: 0–8225–0814–1 (lib. bdg. : alk. paper)
    1. Grant, Ulysses S. (Ulysses Simpson), 1822–1885—Juvenile literature. 2. Presidents—United States—Biography—Juvenile literature. [1. Grant, Ulysses S. (Ulysses Simpson), 1822–1885. 2. Presidents. 3. Generals.] I. Title. II. Series.
    E672.H38   2004
    973.8'2'092—dc22   2003018802

Manufactured in the United States of America
1 2 3 4 5 6 – JR – 09 08 07 06 05 04

CONTENTS

—◇—

INTRODUCTION 7

1 FROM H.U.G. TO UNCLE SAM 10

2 SOLDIER, HUSBAND, FATHER, FAILURE 16

3 "UNCONDITIONAL SURRENDER" GRANT ... 28

4 LIEUTENANT GENERAL, VICTOR 41

5 PEACEKEEPER AND CANDIDATE 54

6 PRESIDENT 67

7 LOYAL AND NAIVE BOSS 81

8 TRAVELER AND AUTHOR 95

TIMELINE 104

SOURCE NOTES 106

BIBLIOGRAPHY 108

FURTHER READING AND WEBSITES 109

INDEX 110

Ulysses S. Grant rose to fame as a brilliant general for the Union in the Civil War (1861–1865).

INTRODUCTION

"In numbers engaged, no such contest ever took place on this continent; in importance of results, but few such have taken place in the history of the world."
—Ulysses S. Grant, referring to the Civil War

General Ulysses S. Grant sat under an oak tree in the dark, soaked by pounding rain. Nearby, wounded Union (Northern) soldiers screamed as their limbs were amputated in makeshift hospital tents. Grant's men had tried and failed to hold off charging Confederate (Southern) rebels that day at a place called Pittsburg Landing, Tennessee.

The Confederates had surprised General Grant's forces, who were waiting for more Northern reinforcements to join them. Confederate general Albert Sidney Johnston didn't want to wait until Grant and the Union army reached full strength. He attacked Grant's troops on Sunday morning, April 6, 1862. The surprise offensive worked—the Confederates pushed Union troops out of their camps and back two miles to the Tennessee River during a brutal daylong battle. A Union soldier named Whitelaw Reid noted, "We have lost nearly all of our camps and camp [supplies]. We have lost nearly half our field artillery . . . our men are discouraged by prolonged defeat."

General Johnston, whom Grant and the Confederacy's president, Jefferson Davis, considered the South's finest officer, bled to death from his wounds during the attack. Johnston's second-in-command, Pierre Beauregard, sent a message to President Davis that he had won "a complete victory" and would finish off Grant's army the next morning.

A Southern soldier named Sam Watkins recalled later that he and others were certain Grant would drop back. "Now those Yankees [Northerners] were whipped, fairly whipped. And according to all the rules of war they ought to have retreated. But they didn't." Instead, Grant and his men waited. Wounded soldiers from both sides lay in the fields, crying for water. Heavy rain began to fall. Grant chose to sleep outside in the thunder and lightning rather than listen to the cries of injured soldiers in his headquarters tent. Soaked from the rain, cigar clamped in his mouth, Grant listened to a Union colonel report that one-third of their troops were out of action and the remaining soldiers were discouraged. When the colonel asked whether he should begin plans for a retreat, Grant seemed taken aback. "Retreat?" Grant said. "No. I propose to attack at daylight and whip them."

Ulysses Grant didn't show his emotions. He just stood his ground. By dawn the long-awaited Union reinforcement troops had arrived. This meant Grant had 50,000 soldiers to the Confederate's 30,000. Early Monday morning, Grant's army went on the attack. By late afternoon, the Confederates retreated.

Ulysses Grant's steadiness and refusal to admit defeat had turned the tide. The Union (the United States) won the bloody battle, which left almost 24,000 soldiers from both sides killed, wounded, or captured. The battle of Pittsburg Landing would come to be known as Shiloh, after the Methodist church near the battleground. More Americans died in two days at Shiloh than had died during the American Revolution (1775–1783), the War of 1812 (1812–1814), and the Mexican War (1846–1848) combined. At Shiloh, as he had in the past and would again in the future, Ulysses S. Grant stood firm, unwavering in what his friend General William Tecumseh Sherman called his "simple faith in success."

───────────────── ✦ ─────────────────

In 1862 Grant and his troops defeated Confederate forces at Shiloh, where close to 25,000 soldiers died.

CHAPTER ONE

FROM H.U.G. TO
UNCLE SAM

*"A military life had no charms for me, and I
had not the faintest idea of staying in the
army even if I should be graduated [from West
Point], which I did not expect."*

—Ulysses S. Grant

Ulysses Grant was born, the first of six Grant children, on
April 27, 1822, in the small town of Point Pleasant, Ohio.
But his parents, Jesse and Hannah Grant, took a few weeks
to decide what to call him. They settled on Hiram Ulysses
Grant. Their shy son was embarrassed about his initials—
H.U.G. He preferred the nickname his family gave him,
Lyss, short for Ulysses.

The young boy loved horses. When he was three years
old, he would swing from the tails of horses. By the time he
was five, the child the world would come to know as Ulysses

S. Grant could ride while standing on top of a horse's back. Soon neighbors would pay him to train their horses.

When he was around eight years old, young Ulysses saw a neighbor's colt he wanted. His father, Jesse, told Ulysses to make a deal with the neighbor and pay up to twenty-five dollars, if necessary, for the colt. Ulysses wasn't skilled at negotiating, so he went to the neighbor and blurted, "Papa says I may offer you twenty dollars for the colt, but if you won't take that, I am to offer twenty-two and a half, and if you won't take that, to give you twenty-five." Not surprisingly, the neighbor ended up getting twenty-five dollars for the colt—and Ulysses got quite a bit of teasing from village boys about his deal.

All Lyss wanted to do was ride horses and help around his family's farm. His father owned a tannery that made leather goods out of horses' hides, but Ulysses swore he'd never work there. He hated to hear the dying horses' cries, and he couldn't stand to see the blood.

Ulysses Grant's birthplace in Ohio

——— ✧ ———

He was sensitive, but he didn't mind hard work. By the time he was eleven, Ulysses recalled, "I was strong enough to hold a plough." He would haul firewood to his family's home and tannery. From age eleven to seventeen, Ulysses was responsible for all the work involving horses—"breaking up the land, furrowing, plowing corn and potatoes, bringing in the crop when harvested, hauling all the wood, besides tending two or three horses, a cow or two, and sawing wood for stoves."

Along with the farmwork, Ulysses went to school. He didn't like it and didn't study much. But Jesse had only had six months of schooling and was determined that his children would receive educations. Jesse and Hannah also believed that as long as their children did their work, they deserved time to play. So Ulysses fished, swam, skated, and rode sleighs. His parents trusted him to be responsible and independent. When he was fifteen, he rode seventy miles by himself on an errand for his father.

Like these boys, Ulysses enjoyed going fishing.

─────── ⬦ ───────

RELUCTANT CADET

When Ulysses was seventeen, Jesse submitted his son's application to go to West Point, the elite military academy in New York State, where the country's top army officials are trained. Ulysses said he didn't want to go. The quiet teenager, who stood just five feet one inch tall and weighed 117 pounds, was afraid he would fail. Jesse gave him little choice. Since Ulysses knew the tannery wasn't his future, he agreed to try the military.

*New York City as it looked when Ulysses visited it
on his way to West Point in 1839*

———————————◇———————————

Getting to West Point gave the young midwesterner the chance to visit what he considered "the two great cities of the continent"—New York and Philadelphia. Traveling alone by train, Ulysses took a scenic route to reach West Point. "I thought the perfection of rapid transit had been reached," he recalled of his train trip. "We traveled at least eighteen miles per hour."

Once he'd seen the sights, Ulysses was ready to go home. He later wrote, "When these places were visited, I would have been glad to have a steamboat or railroad collision, or any other accident happen, by which I might have received a temporary injury sufficient to make me ineligible, for a time, to enter the Academy. Nothing of the kind occurred, and I had to face the music."

The first thing Hiram Ulysses Grant faced at West Point was a paperwork error. The congressman who registered him had mistakenly put Hiram's mother's maiden name, Simpson, as his middle name and his middle name as his first name. Ulysses wanted to switch his name to Ulysses Hiram Grant, to change his embarrassing initials, but West Point stood firm. Since their papers said he was Ulysses Simpson Grant, that's how he would be known. For the rest of his life, he signed his name Ulysses S. Grant.

Fellow cadets (students) quickly nicknamed him "Uncle Sam," in honor of his patriotic initials. Sam Grant liked West Point's drawing and math classes, but not much else. Later, Ulysses would write that he spent more time reading novels than studying. As a cadet, he supported an 1839

In this painting from 1844, picnickers look
up the Hudson River to West Point.

congressional plan to eliminate West Point. The bill failed, and Ulysses didn't do much better. The man who became world famous as America's top general showed little promise when he studied artillery, infantry, and cavalry tactics.

Ulysses decided his goal was to survive the academy and get hired as a math instructor there so he could eventually become a math professor somewhere else. Math wasn't his only strength. Cadet Grant still loved horses. He set a West Point record for a horseback high jump that stood for twenty-five years. Ulysses hoped he'd be assigned to the army's horseback, or cavalry, unit. But he graduated twenty-first in a class of thirty-nine cadets and didn't get that elite assignment.

Instead, Private Grant was assigned to the infantry as a foot soldier. But before he could report for his first tour of duty, he went home to Ohio. He was sick with tuberculosis and had been struggling with "a desperate cough" for six months. Although he'd grown six inches while at West Point, when he was sick, his weight dropped back to 117 pounds, and he thought he might die.

Ulysses was proud to be seen around home in his military clothes—until he realized that people on the streets were making fun of his uniform. Years later, he wrote that being laughed at then "gave me a distaste for military uniform that I never recovered from."

CHAPTER TWO

SOLDIER, HUSBAND, FATHER, FAILURE

"I am almost tempted to resign [from the army] . . . whenever I get to thinking upon the subject however poverty . . . begins to stare me in the face."
—Ulysses S. Grant

Private Ulysses S. Grant reported for duty at Jefferson Barracks, St. Louis, Missouri, on September 30, 1843. Not long after that, he visited a West Point friend, Fred Dent, whose family lived nearby. Grant met Fred's seventeen-year-old sister, Julia, who also loved horses. Soon Julia and Ulysses began taking long rides together. In May, Grant and the rest of the Fourth Infantry were ordered to Louisiana, close to the Texas border. Tensions between the United States and Mexico were rising. Both countries wanted to control Texas, which had been part of Mexico.

Julia Dent, undated engraving
—————————— ✧

Before he left Missouri, the shy army man gave Julia the class ring he wore. She gave him a lock of her hair. The couple secretly became engaged, without her parents' permission. Julia's father didn't want his daughter to marry a soldier.

Once in Louisiana, Grant began writing frequent letters to "My Dear Julia." She replied to her "Ulys." Their love letters buoyed the couple for four years. During this time, Ulysses and Julia would see each other only once. He wrote to her, "You can have but little idea of the influence you have over me Julia, even while so far way . . . and thus it is absent or present I am more or less governed by what I think is your will."

Grant wrote her that he had been offered a job as a math professor in Ohio. But by May 1846, Grant had been promoted, and his regiment was fighting Mexican forces in a war over possession of Texas, California, and much of the land in between. "For myself, a young second lieutenant who had never heard a hostile gun before, I felt sorry that I had enlisted," Grant would write later in his memoirs. The young officer was more interested in love than war. He also believed his side—the United States—was in the wrong. He called the Mexican War (1846–1848) "one of the most unjust ever waged by a stronger against a weaker nation."

Regardless of his personal views, Ulysses Grant followed orders. In Mexico, Grant was assigned to be a quartermaster, the officer in charge of ordering supplies and managing the army pack mules that distributed them. The young second lieutenant didn't want to be separated from his company at the front, but his commanding officer insisted that Grant's skills with animals and numbers made him suited for the quartermaster job. So Grant did as he was told and managed to get his mule trains (groups of mules) to carry supplies where they were needed on time.

✧ ————————————

Ulysses Grant was a second lieutenant and served as quartermaster in the Mexican War (1846–1848).

General Zachary Taylor went on to become president of the United States after the Mexican War.
——————— ✧

Grant looked up to his commander, General Zachary Taylor, who preferred plain clothes to a fancy full-rank uniform and wanted peace rather than war. Young Grant reported that General Taylor was "known to every soldier in his army, and was respected by all."

But Grant believed annexing (claiming) Texas at the beginning of the war, making it part of the United States, only caused greater problems for the country. Northern states, which opposed slavery, didn't want the United States to add new states where people could own slaves. Yet Congress decided slavery would be legal in the new state of Texas. People in the North worried that Texas would then be divided into four slave states, which could tip the balance of power in Congress. If Southern slave states had more members in Congress, they could work to keep slavery legal.

Ulysses and Julia Grant
✧ ————————————

A NEW LIFE

When the Mexican War ended, Grant took a four-month leave of absence and went to St. Louis, where, on August 22, 1848, he married Julia Dent. She was twenty-two; he was twenty-six. The couple spent two years in Detroit, Michigan, where Grant was assigned as quartermaster to the regimental headquarters. In May 1850, their first child, a boy named Frederick Dent Grant, was born. But by spring 1852, when Julia was pregnant again, Grant was headed to the West Coast with the Fourth Infantry. He would again serve as the regimental quartermaster at Fort Vancouver in the Oregon Territory.

Grant tried to add to his meager army salary to support his growing family. He and a partner, Captain Henry Wallen, launched a social club and billiards room. The venture seemed a sure moneymaker, until the business agent they hired to run the club ran off with the profits. Grant and his friend were out of luck. As Captain Wallen recalled, "Neither Grant nor myself had the slightest suggestion of business talent. He was the perfect soul of honor and truth, and believed everyone as artless as himself."

While Grant was stationed in the West, Julia and their son visited Jesse and Hannah Grant for a while and then returned to her parents' home in St. Louis. It would be the first of many separations the army husband and wife would endure. When they were separated, the Grants relied on letters to stay close. On the West Coast, Grant waited for the mail from St. Louis to learn whether Julia had a boy or girl. Four months after the birth, he received Julia's delayed letters, announcing the arrival of their second son, Ulysses Simpson Grant.

——————————— ✧ ———————————

Fort Vancouver in the Oregon Territory, 1848

Hundreds of miles from his family, the lonely officer wrote, "I wish dearest Julia that I could hear from you. . . . If I could only know that you and our little ones were well I would be perfectly satisfied. Kiss them both for me dearest and don't let Fred forget his pa. No person can know the attachment that exists between parent and child until they have been separated for some time. I am almost crazy sometimes to see Fred. I cannot be separated from him and his Ma for a long time."

Grant remained in the West for two years. He was promoted to captain and transferred to remote Fort Humbolt, California, accessible only by boat. There, two hundred miles north of San Francisco, he had little work to keep him busy. He began to drink. His slight build—five feet seven inches, 135 pounds—meant it took little alcohol to get him drunk. A few sips of whiskey made Grant slur his words. Two drinks made him drunk. Reports claimed he was drunk while on duty—drunk while outfitting Captain George B. McClellan's Pacific Coast expedition. Army gossip circulated that the fort's commander forced Captain Grant to resign.

Soldiers assembled at Fort Humboldt
———— ✧ ————

Whatever his reason for resigning, Grant did not write Julia or his father about his decision until May 2, 1854, the day after he was relieved of command. He needed to borrow money from a fellow army man, Simon Bolivar

Buckner, to get home. Grant left California and headed east to Julia. Nine months after he arrived home, their daughter, Ellen Wrenshall Grant, nicknamed Nellie, was born.

CIVILIAN STRUGGLE

Life after the army proved difficult for Grant. Julia's father had given her sixty acres of farmland as a wedding present. The land was in St. Louis, Missouri. The young couple's property was close to White Haven, the Dent family's home. Julia and Ulysses decided to try farming. They named their farm Hardscrabble, which refers to much work for little reward. Grant spent the summer of 1854 clearing land and building a rough log house. He wrote his father asking for a loan of $500. Jesse didn't reply. Another time,

The Grants' first home, Hardscrabble, was in St. Louis, Missouri.

Jesse Grant wrote that he would not lift a finger to help his son as long as Grant continued to live in Missouri, a slave state. Jesse Grant had moved to Ohio from slave-holding Kentucky years earlier, saying he would not live around people who owned slaves.

ULYSSES GRANT AND THE SLAVE ISSUE

Ulysses Grant grew up with a quiet, religious mother and a strong-minded father who did not approve of slavery. Yet he married a Southern woman whose family owned slaves. Ulysses and Julia spent years living in Missouri, a slave-owning state.

At one point, Grant bought a slave named William Jones from Julia's brother, Fred. Grant had thought he would rent Jones out to work for others, while he, as owner, received the salary. Instead, on March 29, 1859, Grant went to court and gave the thirty-five-year-old slave his freedom.

Grant never wrote about why he bought a slave and soon chose to emancipate (free) him. He could have sold William Jones for more than $1,000. The Grants were struggling and in debt. Selling a healthy male slave would have given them enough money to pay off their debts. Perhaps, Ulysses S. Grant was not comfortable selling another human being. He did what he thought right and didn't spend time explaining his actions.

——————————— ✧

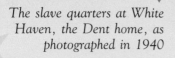

The slave quarters at White Haven, the Dent home, as photographed in 1940

Hardscrabble deserved its name. It took all of Grant's efforts just to survive. The trees he cleared from his fields provided the family's main income. Grant would haul the chopped wood into St. Louis and peddle the firewood on street corners. One day, an army officer who had served with Grant in Mexico saw the scruffy looking thirty-two-year-old. "Good God, Grant, what are you doing?" he asked. Grant answered, "I am solving the problem of poverty."

While selling firewood, Grant ran into other military friends, including another West Point graduate who was down on his luck. His name was William Tecumseh Sherman. The two men agreed that the academy hadn't prepared them for civilian (nonmilitary) life. Another time, Grant saw one of his best friends from West Point, Major James Longstreet. Grant insisted Longstreet take a five-dollar gold piece as payment for a long-forgotten debt. Longstreet tried to refuse, but Grant insisted. "I cannot live with anything in my possession which is not mine," he told his friend.

William Tecumseh Sherman

———— ✧ ————

Desperate for a better job, Grant even tried to get back in the army. Dressed in his faded blue army coat and a worn hat, he applied to be a supply clerk, driving beef cattle across the Great Plains. He didn't get the job.

By 1857 Grant's farm finally seemed on the verge of success. "My oats were good and the corn . . . the best I ever raised," he noted proudly. But those crops went unsold when the country suffered an economic panic and prices fell. That December Grant was forced to pawn his gold pocket watch—his last valuable possession—to buy Christmas presents for his family.

Then Grant was sick for many months with malaria, and by 1858, he and Julia had to give up their dream of farming. That year, the Grants' fourth and last child—Jesse Root Grant—was born. Julia and the children moved into her parents' home, White Haven. Grant got a job with Julia's relative, Harry Boggs, who ran a real estate firm. Grant's job in the firm was to collect rents and keep records. He lived in St. Louis with Harry and his wife, Louise, but would walk twelve miles home to Julia each weekend. Louise Boggs recalled it as a humbling time for Grant. "I never heard him laugh out loud. He was a sad man. I don't believe he had any ambition other than to educate his children and take care of his family."

Even that modest ambition seemed too much for the former soldier. The real estate firm didn't have enough clients to support two families. So, in 1859, Grant left Boggs and struggled to find other work. He was behind in rent and sinking deeper in debt. Grant knew he had no choice. It was time to ask his father for a job in the tannery business. Jesse Grant offered his oldest son $600 a year to work under his two younger brothers in the family's leather goods shop in Galena, Illinois.

In 1860 Ulysses, Julia, and their four children went north to Illinois. They'd had almost seven years of struggle.

Since Grant had swallowed his pride to ask for a job he despised, the family would have enough money. Within a matter of months, the Grants had paid off their debt. Finally, it seemed their life would be safe and stable.

Then in April 1861, news arrived that Southerners had fired on Fort Sumter, a Union fort in South Carolina. One by one, the Southern states had broken away from the United States to form their own nation, where slavery would remain legal. They feared that the recent election of Abraham Lincoln, an antislavery Republican, as president of the United States meant that slavery would not be allowed in any state, North or South.

With the attack on Fort Sumter, the Civil War had begun. Ulysses S. Grant was thirty-eight years old, an unassuming store clerk—but Galena's only West Point graduate. It was natural that Galena residents asked him to organize the volunteers signing up to fight the rebels. Grant helped mobilize the volunteer troops—and never once went back to work in the family store.

——————————✧

The Civil War started in 1861 when Southerners fired on Fort Sumter in South Carolina.

CHAPTER THREE

"UNCONDITIONAL SURRENDER" GRANT

"My heart kept getting higher and higher until it felt to me as though it was in my throat. I would have given anything then to have been back in Illinois, but I had not the moral courage to halt and consider what to do; I kept right on."

—Ulysses S. Grant, describing
his first Civil War battle

Ulysses S. Grant traveled with Galena's volunteer troops to Springfield, the capital of Illinois. But he turned down the chance to be captain of the town's regiment. Instead, he hoped to become a colonel, a commander of a regiment in the regular army, rather than a commander of the volunteers. He wrote to the army, but never heard back. He tried to meet with George B. McClellan, the fellow West Point

graduate who supposedly had seen Grant drunk while outfitting his expedition years earlier in California. When the
Civil War erupted, McClellan was a major general. He
wouldn't meet with Grant.

Still a civilian, Grant considered trying to get a job bak-
ing bread for the army. Instead, Elihu Washburne, a U.S.
congressman from Galena, persuaded the Illinois governor
to appoint Grant the commander of the Twenty-first Illinois
Volunteer Regiment.

After seven years of farming and business, Ulysses S.
Grant was back in the military. Dressed in his frayed civilian
clothes, he went to meet his troops. One Galena merchant,
John Smith, recalled that some soldiers began to mock their
raggedy commander. But Grant
"looked at them just for an instant,
and in that instant they saw they
had a man of nerve to deal with."

Colonel Grant's first job was to
take his regiment to Missouri to
engage the forces of a Confederate
colonel named Thomas Harris in
battle. As his troops traveled along
deserted Southern roads, Grant
grew more nervous about the
enemy ahead. When they reached
Harris's camp, it was deserted. The
Confederate troops had abandoned

———————————— ✧

Grant was nervous about his first
encounter with Confederate colonel
Thomas Harris (right).

the camp on word of a forthcoming attack. Later, Grant would write that he had learned a critical lesson. "From that event to the close of the war, I never experienced trepidation [fear] upon confronting the enemy, though I always felt more or less anxiety. I never forgot that he had as much reason to fear my forces as I had his."

Before fighting a single Civil War battle, Ulysses S. Grant had learned a lesson that would shape his future— and he received a promotion as well. President Lincoln, real- izing the war would last longer than people had first assumed, needed more officers. Colonel Grant was named a brigadier general. In August he took command of about 3,000 inexperienced troops. Grant wrote his father, "All I fear is that too much may be expected of me."

"UNCONDITIONAL SURRENDER"

By February 1862, Grant and his men would give the Union its first big victory over the Confederates. The Union army was positioned near the Kentucky-Tennessee border in the western part of the Confederacy. Both the North and the South wanted to control the key rivers along the Confederacy's western border, which was vital for mov- ing soldiers and supplies into the South.

Brigadier General Grant decided his troops would seize strategic Fort Donelson, on the Cumberland River in Tennessee. About 17,000 Confederates were on duty inside the fort. Grant had about 15,000 soldiers surrounding it, plus several naval vessels in the river. Two of the Union's wooden gunboats and three ironclad battleships attacked the fort, but they were damaged and had to pull back. When Grant went downriver to meet with an injured naval commander, Confederates ran from the fort. Union troops panicked—thinking the Confederates were attacking—and began falling back.

Grant raced back to the fort on his horse to rally his troops. "Fill your cartridge boxes, quick, and get in line," he commanded. "The enemy is trying to escape and he must not be permitted to do so." Later, Grant would write that his quick rally "worked like a charm. The men only wanted someone to give them a command."

Grant's cool head turned what might have become a Union defeat into victory. Although some Confederate troops and cavalry escaped, most Confederates remained trapped inside the fort. Confederate general Simon Bolivar Buckner, the former West Point friend of Grant, asked what surrender terms the Union expected. Grant's no-nonsense written reply would make him famous: "No terms except an immediate and unconditional surrender can be accepted. I propose to move immediately upon your works [fort]."

——————————— ✦ ———————————

Union and Confederate troops fight for control of Fort Donelson in 1862.

A SQUEAMISH SOLDIER

Ulysses S. Grant earned his reputation as a tough and fearless general. But he had another side as well. Grant was shy. He had kept a journal at West Point, and when it was lost, he spent years worrying that it would be found and that other people would read his private thoughts. He always bathed in a closed tent so that no one would see him naked.

He also hated the thought of animals suffering. He refused to eat chicken, saying he could never eat something that walked on two legs. The meat he would eat had to be cooked until it was dry. Even a hint of blood in his meat would make him sick. Once, the night before a fierce battle, he had a Union man tied to a tree for six hours because the man had mistreated a horse.

Grant hated making speeches. When the Union general first met Andrew Johnson (the military governor of Tennessee who would later become Lincoln's vice president and then president), Grant stood, sweating and listening to Johnson's long-winded speech. Johnson was welcoming Grant to Nashville. "I was in torture while he [Johnson] was delivering it, fearing something would be expected from me in response," Grant wrote later.

The general some critics later called a butcher hated to see war. After surveying the battle scene at Fort Donelson, he told his chief of staff, "Let's get away from this dreadful place. I suppose this work is part of the devil that is left in us all." After that same battle, Grant was overheard quoting Scottish poet Robert Burns to himself: "Man's inhumanity to man/Makes countless thousands mourn." And yet this squeamish man, who could not abide the sight of blood, was brave. One time, as he sat writing orders on a hillside near a battle, a shell exploded by Grant. The general didn't flinch. A nearby soldier remarked, "Ulysses don't scare worth a damn."

The Confederate general had no choice but to accept what he called Grant's "ungenerous and unchivalrous" conditions. Buckner had wanted Grant to appoint a commission to decide on terms of surrender. Grant wasn't interested in a commission or anything less than total surrender. Northern schoolchildren memorized Grant's letter. Newspapers nicknamed the young brigadier general Unconditional Surrender Grant.

Grant offered Confederate general Buckner money to get home, just as Buckner had done for him years earlier when Grant resigned from the army in California. And Grant refused to allow an official surrender ceremony that would rub defeat into the Confederates' faces. "Why," he asked, "should we go through vain forms and mortify and injure the spirit of brave men, who, after all, are our own countrymen?"

U. S. Grant was famous. He was the first American general since George Washington to capture an entire enemy army in the field. President Lincoln quickly promoted Grant to major general. Newspapers detailed General Grant's "deep thought, extreme determination, and great calmness." Reporters described small details, including how the general chomped an unlit cigar. Northerners, grateful for the victory, began deluging the general with cigars. Grant preferred smoking a clay pipe and, at first, gave away many of the cigars, but he received nearly ten thousand boxes of them. Soon he was smoking about twenty cigars a day.

The relatively easy victory at Fort Donelson convinced Grant that the Union would soon defeat the rebels. He wanted to follow up quickly on his first success by heading deeper into enemy territory. But his persistence hit a

Major General Henry Halleck
──── ✧ ────

major obstacle. Grant's boss, Major General Henry Halleck, was afraid Grant would grab all the Union's glory. Halleck tried to rein in Grant. He spread rumors that Grant was drinking again.

Halleck grew angry when he didn't get Grant's field reports. At first, neither general knew the reason—Grant's telegraph operator was a Confederate spy, who stole the messages. Grant, the Union's first big victor, was close to being arrested for disobeying his superior officer. It wasn't until the telegraph operator abandoned his post, taking the dispatches with him, that the Union learned what he was doing, and Halleck realized why communication had broken down. Within a few weeks, the two military men resolved their misunderstandings. Grant set his sights on the enemy.

SHILOH

When the problem with General Halleck was settled, Grant and his troops were sent to join forces with another Union army. But while Grant's forces camped on the west bank of the Tennessee River at Pittsburg Landing, disaster struck.

Confederate General Albert Sidney Johnston had secretly moved about 40,000 rebel soldiers close to the Union camps.

On the morning of April 6, 1862, Confederate troops attacked Grant's army of 42,000 men. By 9 A.M., they had wiped out a Union division. By day's end, rebels controlled three of the Union's five camps. Close to 7,000 Union troops lay dead or wounded. Another 3,000 had been captured. But the Confederates had suffered as well. General Johnston had been shot and killed—he would be the highest-ranking officer from either side to die in the Civil War.

That night Grant sat in the drenching rain, too sickened by the sight of blood to stay inside tents where doctors treated wounded and dying soldiers. He was heard muttering, "Not beaten yet. Not by a damn sight." Fellow Union general William Tecumseh Sherman went to Grant intending to ask him to retreat across the river. Sherman saw Grant's resolve and didn't ask. Instead, Sherman said, "Well, Grant, we've had the devil's own day, haven't we?" Calmly, Grant replied, "Yes. Lick 'em tomorrow though." Grant told his friend that the situation was like the one at Fort Donelson—victory would go to whichever side took the offensive.

Overnight, some 20,000 troops arrived to bolster Grant's army. The Union went on the offense. By 2 P.M., the Confederates were ready to retreat. Of the 100,000 men at Shiloh, almost one-fourth—23,746—were killed, wounded, or captured. More soldiers died at Shiloh than in all of America's previous wars combined. After the battle, Grant surveyed the open field, "so covered with dead that it would have been possible to walk across the clearing, in any direction, stepping on dead bodies, without a foot touching the ground." The bloody victory forced Grant to see that the Confederates would not surrender easily. From then on, General Grant knew the Union would need total victory to defeat the South.

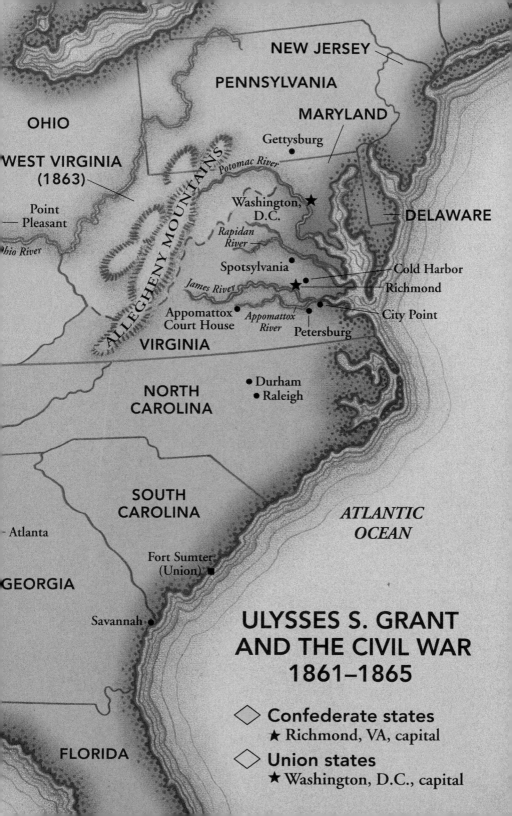

NEW JERSEY

PENNSYLVANIA

OHIO

MARYLAND

Gettysburg

WEST VIRGINIA
(1863)

Potomac River

Point
Pleasant

Washington,
D.C.

DELAWARE

hio River

*Rapidan
River*

Spotsylvania

Cold Harbor

Richmond

James River

City Point

Appomattox
Court House

*Appomattox
River*

Petersburg

VIRGINIA

NORTH
CAROLINA

Durham
Raleigh

ALLEGHENY MOUNTAINS

SOUTH
CAROLINA

ATLANTIC
OCEAN

Atlanta

Fort Sumter
(Union)

GEORGIA

Savannah

ULYSSES S. GRANT
AND THE CIVIL WAR
1861–1865

FLORIDA

◇ **Confederate states**
★ Richmond, VA, capital

◇ **Union states**
★ Washington, D.C., capital

Grant's troops held their ground at Shiloh, but some began calling Grant a butcher, too willing to send his troops to die. In one month, nearly 45,000 men of Grant's 118,000 soldiers had been killed or wounded. When critics demanded that Grant be fired, President Lincoln stood firmly behind his determined general, saying, "I can't spare this man; he fights."

VICKSBURG

In July 1862, Grant was put in command of the Army of the Tennessee, which included all of the Union forces west of the Tennessee River. Near the end of the year, Grant began his next major assault. He intended to capture Vicksburg, Mississippi, a river town that Confederate president Jefferson Davis called "the nailhead that [holds] the South's two halves together." The North had taken control of some parts of the Mississippi River farther south. But Vicksburg, set three hundred feet above the Mississippi, provided a strategic spot for the South to maintain control over this crucial waterway.

At first General Grant tried attacking Vicksburg directly, but it was too difficult for troops to enter the city high above the river. So Grant decided to have his men encircle the port and block supplies from reaching the city. The siege of Vicksburg lasted two and a half months. Trapped Southerners in Vicksburg ran out of food and ended up killing and eating their horses—and even the rats. Northern newspapers criticized Grant for not attacking, saying he had lost his nerve. But Grant held his ground. On July 4, 1863, Vicksburg surrendered. The Civil War would drag on for another year

A Union soldier from Illinois said that charges on Vicksburg were
"like marching men to their graves in line of battle."

——————— ✧ ———————

and a half, but to Grant, "The fate of the Confederacy
was sealed when Vicksburg fell. Much hard fighting was
to be done afterwards and many precious lives were to
be sacrificed; but the morale was with the supporters of
the Union ever after."

Grant with his favorite horse, Cincinnati

CHAPTER FOUR

LIEUTENANT GENERAL, VICTOR

"I felt like anything rather than rejoicing at the downfall of a foe who had fought so long and valiantly."
—Ulysses S. Grant, at the end of the Civil War

In August 1863, Grant's horse was spooked by a train and fell on top of him. Grant collapsed, unconscious, and woke later in a hotel room with doctors examining him. "My leg was swollen from the knee to the thigh, and the swelling, almost to the point of bursting, extended along the body to the arm-pit. The pain was almost beyond endurance," he wrote later. It took days before Grant could turn over in bed. The injury sidelined him for weeks. In his entire military career, this incident would be Grant's worst injury.

While he was recuperating, Grant was named commander of the Military Division of the Mississippi. He was responsible for all of the Union forces in a huge swath of land stretching from the Allegheny Mountains to the Mississippi River. When he recovered, General Grant quickly used his newly expanded army to defeat the Confederates at Chattanooga, Tennessee.

In January 1864, Grant went home to St. Louis, Missouri, to see his oldest son, thirteen-year-old Fred, who was seriously ill. Fred and the rest of the family had been with Grant after the siege of Vicksburg, and the boy had become sick then. Fred eventually recovered.

General Grant's victories at Vicksburg and Chattanooga spurred Northerners to consider him as a presidential candidate for the 1864 election. But Grant had no desire to replace President Lincoln in the White House. He said so plainly in a letter to an Illinois congressman: "This is the last thing in the world I desire. I would regard such a consummation [result] as being highly unfortunate for myself, if not for the country. Through Providence [God's care] I have attained to more than I had ever hoped and . . . infinitely prefer my present position to that of any civil office within the gift of the people."

A grateful Lincoln wanted to reward Grant, who had accomplished more than any other Union general. So in March 1864, the president promoted him to Lieutenant General of the Army, making him commander of all Union forces. George Washington had been the only American to hold that post—until Ulysses S. Grant.

For the promotion ceremony, Grant and Fred took the train to Washington, D.C. They walked into the Willard Hotel, where Grant asked for a room. The hotel clerk, looking at the dusty, inconspicuous pair, replied with a

This document
with Lincoln's signature
made Grant's promotion
to lieutenant general of
the army official.
——————————— ❖

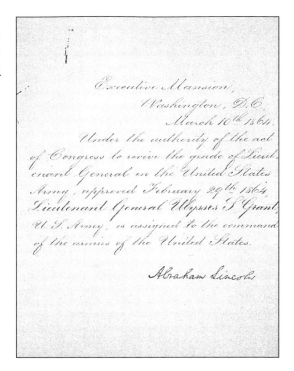

sneer that the only opening was a small attic room. Fancy quarters didn't mean much to the modest general. He said that the small room was fine and signed the register, "U. S. Grant and son, Galena, Illinois." When the clerk saw Grant's name, he immediately offered the presidential suite and carried Grant's bags up there himself.

Grant wasn't comfortable being the center of attention. But that night, at a White House reception, so many people wanted a glimpse of this famous military man that his boss, Secretary of War Edwin Stanton, had Grant stand on a sofa so that everyone could see him. One congressman recalled, "The little, scared-looking man who stood on a crimson-colored sofa was the idol of the hour."

The reception was the first time Lincoln met Grant in person. The two plainspoken men from Illinois quickly established a rapport. At the formal ceremony the next day, Grant told Lincoln and the audience, "I feel the full weight of the responsibilities now devolving on me; and I know that if they are met, it will be due to those armies, and above all, to the favor of that Providence which leads both nations and men."

Most top generals oversee wars from headquarters far from the action. But that wasn't the way Grant wanted to run his army of 533,000 men. He had no interest in Washington politics. He intended to stay close to the action, explaining, "The distant rear of an army engaged in battle is not the best place from which to judge correctly what is going on in front."

Ulysses Grant's memoirs make it clear he did judge correctly what was going on in front—and he could spell out the situation in concise terms. He wrote, "When I assumed command of all the armies the situation was about this: the Mississippi River was guarded [by Union forces]

Grant liked to stay close to the action, where he put his field glasses (binoculars) to good use.

from St. Louis to its mouth; the line of the Arkansas [River] was held, thus giving us all the North-west north of that river. . . . West Virginia was in our hands. . . . The balance of the Southern territory, an empire in extent, was still in the hands of the enemy."

Grant's orders to his generals were clean, simple, and direct. No one could mistake his meaning. He had two main goals—first, to capture Confederate general Robert E. Lee at the Southern capital of Richmond, Virginia; second, to capture Confederate general Joseph Johnston and the Southern port of Atlanta. The rest of the war would be spent trying to achieve those two goals.

BATTLE OF THE WILDERNESS

On May 5, 1864, the armies of Ulysses Grant and Robert E. Lee met for the first time in dark and jumbled underbrush by the Rapidan River in Virginia. The Battle of the Wilderness was a mess—whole units of soldiers became lost. Unable to see more than fifty feet ahead, they ended up firing on their own men. Troops camped in woods where the bones of soldiers who had died a year earlier jutted out from the ground. Grant described the Wilderness campaign "as desperate fighting as the world has ever witnessed."

About 17,000 Union soldiers and 11,000 Confederates died in the first two days of the Wilderness battle. Sparks from ammunition ignited brushfires, burning 200 wounded soldiers. The night of May 6, Ulysses Grant went to his tent and broke down and cried. But the next day, instead of retreating, Grant ordered his men to march forward. Union soldiers cheered. They, like their commander,

After the Wilderness battle in Virginia, as in other Civil War battles, the exhausted survivors buried the dead.

───────────────────── ◇ ─────────────────────

understood that the only way to end the Civil War was to defeat Lee and capture Richmond. Fellow Union general Philip Sheridan called Grant's decision to advance after his Wilderness defeat, "the supreme moment of his life."

Grant and his Army of the Potomac, the largest of the Union armies, would spend six brutal weeks doggedly trying to get past Robert E. Lee's right flank (side) to reach Richmond. Union and rebel troops clashed at Spotsylvania, Virginia, where 12,000 soldiers from both sides died before General Lee pulled back. On May 11, Grant wrote to Lincoln, "I propose to fight it out on this line if it takes all summer."

"I REGRET THIS ASSAULT"

Grant tried attacking Lee's forces head on at Cold Harbor, a small town northeast of Richmond. Northern troops knew it was a suicide mission. The night before the battle, veteran soldiers quietly wrote their names and addresses on scraps of paper that they pinned to their coats, so their bodies could be identified after they died. On the morning of June 2, 1864, Union soldiers charged the heavily fortified rebel positions. About 7,000 Union men died—most in the first hour of battle. Generals Grant and Lee each refused to call for a truce. For three days, thousands of wounded soldiers lay dying in the hot Virginia sun. One injured man was seen slitting his own throat. By the time medics went to recover the injured, only two of the thousands of wounded Union soldiers were still alive. "The dead covered more than five acres of ground about as thickly as they could be laid," one colonel wrote. Later, Grant apologized to his staff, saying, "I regret this assault more than any I have ever ordered."

Union general Philip Sheridan
——————— ✧ ———————

The senseless deaths at Cold Harbor convinced Grant he needed a new tactic. Instead of trying to outflank Lee, Grant decided to bypass Richmond completely. He ordered 115,000 troops to sneak south of Richmond by crossing the James River into Petersburg. By mid-June, Grant had set up a new field headquarters at City Point, Virginia, on a bluff overlooking the Appomattox and James rivers.

A GENERAL'S LIFE

Ulysses S. Grant—the highest-ranking American general since George Washington—didn't stand on ceremony. He wore a simple uniform, with just the general's bars on his lapels. His plain clothes gave him freedom when he was traveling. Civilians assumed that Grant's medical director, a distinguished-looking gray-haired man, was the general. While grateful civilians swarmed the doctor, General Grant was happy to be ignored.

Grant didn't like big parades and formal ceremonies, either. He said he only knew two tunes. "One is 'Yankee Doodle'; the other isn't." He kept his dealings with his small staff casual. Even as the army's top commander, he chose to have just fourteen officers on his staff. Two staff members worked in Washington, D. C., while Grant and the others stayed in the field.

Grant's field headquarters consisted of three tents—a large hospital tent that also functioned as the mess quarters where officers ate, a business tent for staff meetings, and Grant's small personal tent. His quarters were spartan, containing a cot, a tin washbasin, one small trunk, two camp chairs, and a simple table. The general's meals were as plain as his clothes. Breakfast was black coffee and sliced cucumbers with vinegar. He also liked buckwheat pancakes and pork and beans.

✧ ————————

Grant's name is etched on this field lantern, which he used during the war. A lantern as decorative as this one would have been a gift from an admirer.

Although he reportedly was drunk at least once during the Civil War, no accurate accounts claim that he drank during battle. His chief of staff, John Rawlins, a friend from Galena, was believed to have kept Grant from alcohol.

His one extravagance, aside from the many cigars Northerners sent, was horses. Grant had at least five horses at different times during the war. One pony, named Jeff Davis, had been taken from the plantation of Confederate president Jefferson Davis's brother. Grant's favorite steed, Cincinnati, was a gift from a St. Louis man after the Chattanooga victory. Cincinnati was an offspring of the fastest racing Thoroughbred in the country. After the war, Grant refused an offer of $10,000 for his favorite horse.

———————————— ◇ ————————————

(Left to right) *Grant's horses Egypt, Cincinnati, and Jeff Davis*

Grant's City Point headquarters was some distance from battle, and officers had cabins. Some, such as Grant's chief of staff John Rawlins (left), enjoyed a family visit while they were camped there.

✧ ————————————————

Establishing the City Point headquarters allowed Grant to reunite with his wife. Julia and their youngest son, Jesse, came and stayed with the general. The older children were in school. Grant said he always felt more comfortable when Julia was with him. She was grateful once again to be with her husband. On calm evenings, the couple would sit holding hands, and if one of Grant's officers walked in and saw them, "they would look as bashful as two young lovers spied upon in the scenes of their courtship," one aide recalled. But when Julia asked to go visit an old friend, the wife of Confederate general James Longstreet, Grant said no. It was absurd, he said, that his wife wanted to meet with a Confederate in the midst of war.

On June 20, President Lincoln and his son Tad paid a visit to Grant at City Point. "I just thought I would jump aboard a boat and come down and see you," Lincoln told his top commander. "I don't expect I can do any good, and in fact I may do harm but I'll put myself under your orders and if you find me doing anything wrong just send me [off] right away," Lincoln told Grant. The two men told stories, visited the troops, and rode horseback. Grant let the president ride his favorite mount, Cincinnati.

Lincoln felt comfortable with Grant, but both men knew the president's fate hinged on the war effort. Lincoln needed Union victories if he was to be reelected in November. At Petersburg, Grant and his Southern opponent, General Lee, would stand off for ten months. It was Grant's most trusted general, William Tecumseh Sherman, who gave Lincoln the victory that led to his reelection. While Grant kept Lee trapped at Petersburg, Sherman captured and burned Atlanta in the autumn of 1864. In the following months, his troops moved through Georgia, leaving a forty-mile-wide path of destruction in his "March to the Sea."

By spring 1865, the South was running out of men, weapons, time, and hope. On March 3, 1865, Lee wrote Grant asking to meet. Grant passed the message to Washington, D.C., where Lincoln decided the two generals

——————————— ✧ ———————————

During Sherman's famous March to the Sea, Union soldiers raided Confederate homes and tore up enemy railroad tracks.

could meet only about military matters. Lee was desperate. His only chance was to link up with Confederate general Joseph Johnston, who was one hundred miles south. Lee and his army took to the road, leaving Richmond to fall to Union forces. Grant pursued Lee and cut off the Confederates near the small town of Amelia Courthouse, Virginia.

On April 7, 1865, Grant seemed to surprise himself when he told his fellow generals, "I have a great mind to summon Lee to surrender." Lee replied to the letter calling for surrender, asking what terms the Union wanted. Grant wrote back, "Peace being my great desire, there is but one condition I would insist upon: namely, the men and officers surrendered shall be disqualified from taking up arms against the Government of the United States."

Lee wasn't ready to quit. Although his army was desperately hungry and outnumbered almost four to one, the Confederate general planned to attack on April 9. But that morning, Palm Sunday, Lee and his soldiers saw they were surrounded by Union troops. There was no way out. Lee's 17,000 haggard survivors were no match for Grant's 125,000 troops. Lee told his staff, "There is nothing left for me to do but to go and see General Grant, and I would rather die a thousand deaths."

By noon of Palm Sunday, Lee sent Grant a letter saying he would surrender. The two generals agreed to meet at a house in Appomattox Court House, Virginia, on April 12, 1865. Robert E. Lee came wearing his full-dress uniform, resplendent in red silk sash, ornate sword, and scabbard. He assumed he would become a Union prisoner. Ulysses Grant showed up in muddy boots and a faded uniform borrowed from a private. "Unconditional Surrender" Grant seemed anything but the triumphant victor. He wrote later that he felt sad and depressed to see the downfall of his enemy. His terms for surrender were brief and generous.

"The war is over," Grant said. "The rebels are our countrymen again." He let Lee go free and said that Confederates who agreed to surrender their weapons could go home in peace. He allowed Southern soldiers to keep their horses to use in their fields back home. He offered food for the starving rebels who had been living on the dried corn they kept to feed the horses.

Grant stopped Union troops who began firing victory salutes. He didn't want to rub defeat in his countrymen's faces. He chose not to go through Richmond on his way back to Washington, D. C., saying, "We ought not to do anything at such a time which would add to their sorrow."

Ulysses S. Grant had won the war. It was time to begin making peace.

——————— ✧
Grant (left) was not this well dressed when he accepted Lee's (right) surrender at Appomattox Court House, Virginia. Most artwork depicting the surrender, such as this etching, dresses Grant up.

CHAPTER FIVE

PEACEKEEPER AND CANDIDATE

"Let us have peace."
—Ulysses S. Grant

When the news of Robert E. Lee's surrender to Ulysses Grant reached Washington, D. C., the capital erupted in celebration. Cannons roared, steam whistles blared, and marching bands boomed "Yankee Doodle," "The Battle Hymn of the Republic," and "The Star Spangled Banner." President Lincoln asked to hear the Confederate anthem, "Dixie," a song he said he always liked. Lincoln, like Grant, wanted generous terms for the people of the South. No one knew how peace would work.

For four years, the country had been tangled in war. It was time to think about making peace. Ulysses Grant chose not to stay at Appomattox for the formal surrender ceremony on April 12, 1865. He had to attend to stopping the machinery of war. He traveled all night from City Point, Virginia, to Washington, D.C., and arrived at the capital the morning of April 13. At army headquarters, he told his staff to stop buying war supplies and begin discharging injured soldiers who were well enough to go home. The Civil War, which had ended up costing $4 million a day, was history.

That night, Grant and Lincoln toured Washington, watching "a grand illumination," the lighting of all the capital's public buildings. Everywhere they went, the two men,

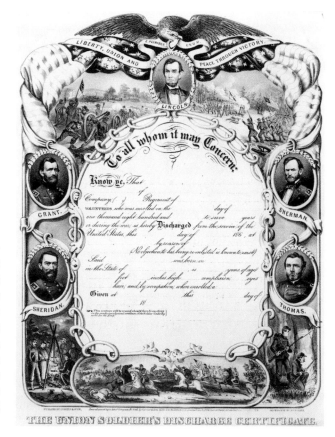

A Union soldier's discharge certificate featured (from the top, clockwise) portraits of President Abraham Lincoln and generals William T.Sherman, George H. Thomas, Philip Sheridan, and Grant.

president and general, were cheered. The next morning, Good Friday, April 14, Grant attended a cabinet meeting at the White House. Lincoln invited Grant and his wife to attend a play that Mrs. Lincoln wanted to see. But Julia, who didn't like Mary Todd Lincoln, told her husband that she wanted to visit their children, who were staying in New Jersey. So that evening, the Grants took a north-bound train. When they stopped in Philadelphia, a telegram awaited them: "THE PRESIDENT WAS ASSASSINATED AT FORD'S THEATER AT 10:30 TONIGHT AND CANNOT LIVE. . . . THE SECRETARY OF STATE DESIRES THAT YOU RETURN TO WASHINGTON IMMEDIATELY."

Grant would later call April 14 "the darkest day in my life." He blamed himself for not being at Ford's Theatre with Lincoln, for not being able to stop the assassination. The next day, the grief-stricken general headed back to Washington, D.C., alone. He took no escort or bodyguard. Grant helped organize parts of Lincoln's funeral and ordered that an African American regiment be included in the honor guard (the guards who accompany a casket in a military funeral).

When Lincoln's body lay in state in the White House, Grant stood alone at the head of the coffin, crying. Grant had become a friend of the president. He cried for the loss of his friend and for what that loss would mean for the country. He told Julia, "The President was inclined to be kind and [generous], and his death at this time is an irreparable loss to the South." The general worried about how Lincoln's successor, the newly sworn-in President Andrew Johnson, would reconstruct the country after the war had officially ended. General Grant's job would be to help enforce peaceful reconstruction after the war was officially ended.

New Yorkers watch Lincoln's funeral procession pass. The train carrying Lincoln's body home from Washington, D.C., for burial in Springfield, Illinois, made many such stops.

❖

At first, Grant feared the new president would be too harsh on Southerners. As a senator and then vice president, Johnson had accused his fellow Southerners of treason for rebelling against the Union. But President Johnson began his administration trying to walk a fine line between Radical Republicans, who wanted to punish the South, and Southern Democrats, who wanted to maintain control over their former slaves. President Johnson would need the support of powerful allies like Ulysses Grant.

Later in April 1865, Grant traveled south to Raleigh, North Carolina, to meet with Union general William Sherman about the surrender of Confederate general Joseph Johnston. Sherman and Johnston ended up signing a peace accord similar to the one Grant had written at Appomattox.

The trip to Raleigh gave Grant time to observe the ravaged South. "The suffering that must exist in the South . . . even with the war ending now, will be beyond conception," he wrote to Julia. "People who talk of further retaliation and punishment, except of the political leaders, either do not conceive of the suffering endured already or they are heartless and unfeeling."

Grant believed that "management is all that is now wanted to secure complete peace." The general did what he could to manage that peace. He recommended temporarily dividing the South into several military districts, which could be supervised by Union forces. Some of Grant's top generals, like Philip Sheridan, would enforce the peace.

In Washington, D.C., Grant was forced to deal with politics. In June 1865, he threatened to quit the army if the

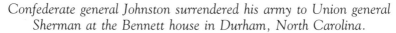

Confederate general Johnston surrendered his army to Union general Sherman at the Bennett house in Durham, North Carolina.

government went ahead with plans to try Robert E. Lee for treason. Grant believed the treaty at Appomattox protected Lee and other Confederate officers from prosecution. The country's top general and its president were both stubborn. But President Johnson knew he needed Grant. The president agreed to let Robert E. Lee remain free.

After four years of war, Ulysses Grant was tired. He took time off during the summer of 1865 to be with his family and escape the politics of Washington. His family's hometown of Galena, Illinois, donated a house, completely furnished, to Ulysses and Julia. Wealthy supporters also donated a town house in Philadelphia, where Grant hoped to live and commute to Washington, D. C. But Grant soon realized that his job as commander, even in peacetime, demanded that he be in Washington. He and Julia settled there in a house on I Street, paid for by a friend from Missouri. Wealthy investors gave the Grants $105,000. For once, Ulysses and Julia were together and had money.

(Front row, left to right) *Jesse, Ulysses Jr., and Julia;* (back) *Nellie, Frederick, and Grant*

─────── ✧ ───────

At his army headquarters, Grant worked to shrink the nation's military. By November 1865, the U.S. armed forces had been cut from one million men to 183,000.

Although the fighting had ceased, racial tensions remained high. In the South, African Americans faced lynchings and death threats from the Ku Klux Klan and other secret societies. These groups had been formed by angry white Southerners to discourage former slaves from fully enjoying the benefits of freedom. President Johnson sent Grant south to report on the situation. Grant spent two weeks in late 1865 visiting Virginia, Tennessee, the Carolinas, and Georgia. On December 6, the Thirteenth Amendment to the Constitution, outlawing slavery, was ratified (made into law).

A SYMBOLIC PARTY

One evening in April 1866, Ulysses and Julia Grant hosted a grand party. President Johnson, who normally didn't attend social gatherings at night, came to the Grants' home, as did Alexander Stephens, who had been the Confederacy's vice president. The Grants' expansive guest list was a sign that they hoped people from the North and South could get along together. The party was a success. Alexander Stephens even shook hands with Thaddeus Stevens, leader of the Radical Republicans—congressmen demanding equal rights for African Americans and punishment for Southern whites. Although guests at the Grants' party were cordial, tensions between Northerners and Southerners remained.

The day the Grants hosted their party, Congress over-rode President Johnson's veto of a civil rights bill. The bill, which states later ratified as the Fourteenth Amendment, gave African Americans who were born in the United States the same rights as white Americans. They could buy and sell property, make contracts, and sue. It didn't say anything about the right to vote. Johnson believed the bill gave African Americans preferential treatment, and he refused to support it. For his part, General Grant firmly believed African Americans deserved the rights listed in the bill. But in the South, they were getting far less than the equality it called for.

On May 1, 1866, a race riot broke out in Memphis, Tennessee, killing forty-six people—forty-four of whom were African Americans. After more bloodshed in Mississippi in July, General Grant sent four companies of cavalry to stop the violence. He issued general orders giving all army commanders in the South the power to arrest civilians for crimes if the police and other civil authorities failed to act. But later that same month, police in New Orleans, Louisiana, killed forty-eight more African Americans who were demonstrating for civil rights.

A procession of African Americans (center) *carrying an American flag meets white opposition* (bottom) *in New Orleans, Louisiana.*

In August Grant and the entire presidential cabinet, except War Secretary Edwin Stanton, joined President Johnson in a tour of the country. The president hoped his "Swing Around the Circle" tour would sway voters to support him in the upcoming presidential election and help him win the next election. But crowds clamored for "Grant, Grant, Grant." The general didn't agree with the president's racist policies and didn't want to say anything that would help Johnson win. He wrote Julia, "I have never been so tired of anything before as I have with the political stump speeches of Mr. Johnson. I look

President Andrew Johnson
————— ✧ —————

upon them as a National disgrace." Grant was fed up with Johnson's hateful racist speeches. He claimed to be sick and left the presidential tour early.

POLITICAL WARFARE

The tension between General Grant and President Johnson would grow far worse. Grant believed the president's harsh attitude toward African Americans was preventing the country from healing. The men's relationship further soured in August 1867, when Johnson tried to force War Secretary

Stanton out of office. The president wanted Grant to take the job. Grant didn't want to help push out his boss. But Johnson suspended Stanton, and Grant agreed to be acting secretary of war. In February 1868, when Congress voted to back Stanton, Grant stepped down. President Johnson was livid. He accused Grant of tricking him. Grant, who was politically naive and known for his honesty, was offended. The two men exchange bitter letters, which ended up in the newspapers. The *New York Independent* newspaper noted, "General Grant has driven his pen through the President like a spear."

War Secretary Edwin Stanton
────── ✧ ──────

Members of Congress were outraged that the president had suspended War Secretary Stanton. Congress had passed the Tenure of Office Act on March 2, 1867, requiring presidents to tell Congress in writing about the dismissal of any cabinet officer. Johnson had suspended Stanton when Congress was adjourned (not in session), so the president thought he didn't have to notify them. Congress disagreed. On February 24, 1868, the House of Representatives voted to impeach (charge) President Johnson with wrongdoing. At the Senate trial, the vote was close. Johnson was not convicted and remained in office. But he had no chance of being reelected in November. As the presidential election neared, the nation turned its hope toward an untarnished hero—Ulysses S. Grant.

A QUIET CANDIDATE

Ulysses Grant was no stump speaker. He hated making speeches and wasn't any good at it. He had no interest in making his private thoughts public. Few people knew whether he wanted to be president—or would even consider being a candidate. Still, when the Republican convention met in Chicago on May 20, 1868, Ulysses Grant was the only candidate nominated. Grant didn't attend the convention. He was back in Washington, D. C., at work in the War Department. The next day, Grant made his first political speech, noting, "All I can say is, that to whatever position I may be called by your will, I shall endeavor to discharge its duties with fidelity and honesty of purpose." A week later, with one hundred supporters watching, Grant and Republican vice presidential candidate Schuyler Colfax accepted their party's nomination. The following day, Grant wrote a simple letter stating his support for the Republican platform (list of objectives). He signed his letter with four words that would become the rallying cry for his election bid: "Let us have peace."

That brief statement would be Grant's last words concerning the presidential campaign of 1868. He went back to work as commander in chief, then toured western forts before returning to Galena, Illinois, with Julia. There he stayed, avoiding politics as much as possible, until November 3, 1868. On that election day, Ulysses Grant went to the polls and voted—but he chose not to cast any vote for president.

Despite his nonvote, Grant easily won election, defeating Democrat Horatio Seymour by more than 300,000 votes. He had spent election night playing cards with friends, and when the vote outcome was clear, he went home to Julia, saying, "I am afraid I am elected." The shy midwestern boy, who had failed as an army captain, failed as a farmer, failed as a small businessman, was to be the eighteenth president of the United States.

——————— ✧

"Let us Preserve [the Union] at the Ballot-Box" (near right) *is a slogan Grant's supporters used. In contrast, hostile racism* (far right) *characterized the campaign of his opponent Horatio Seymour.*

OUR CHOICE.

For President,
ULYSSES S. GRANT.
For Vice-President,
SCHUYLER COLFAX.

We Saved the Union in the Field—Let us Preserve it at the Ballot-Box.

Entered according to Act of Congress, in the year 1868, by Benjamin W. Hitchcock, in the Clerk's Office of the District Court of the United States for the Southern District of New York.

OUR TICKET.

For President   Vice President

SEYMOUR   BLAIR

OUR MOTTO:
THIS IS A WHITE MAN'S COUNTRY: LET WHITE MEN RULE.

Entered according to Act of Congress A. D. 1868, by B. W. Hitchcock, in the Clerk's Office of the District Court for the Southern Dist. of New York.

Grant's first inaugural ball was held in a big building that may have been
a temporary hospital for treating wounded soldiers during the Civil War.

CHAPTER SIX

PRESIDENT

*"If the men who have to do the fighting could
have the management in time of peace, they
would most likely preserve peace, for their own
comfort if for no other reason."*

—Ulysses Grant

When Ulysses S. Grant took the oath of office on March 4, 1869, he was forty-six years old—the youngest president the United States had had. During his inaugural speech, his thirteen-year-old daughter, Nellie, ran up to her father and held his hand. The crowd exploded in cheers. The country was looking forward to its new young leader—the most popular American general since George Washington.

Like Washington, President Grant had little experience with politics. He was not tied closely to a party. He had no experience in government and had never before been elected to office. He promised to "have no policy of my own to interfere against the will of the people." Grant believed Congress should set policy, and the president and his administration should carry it out.

Many of the men Grant chose for his cabinet had little experience in the office to which they were named. President Grant did not discuss his cabinet appointments before announcing them. He simply chose people with whom he could work. His old army buddy from Galena, John Rawlins, who was dying of tuberculosis, became secretary of war. He named Illinois congressman Elihu B. Washburne, who had helped get him his first Civil War appointment, as secretary of state. But Washburne had no experience and was forced to resign less than a week later. Washburne became the U.S. minister to France, and a New Yorker named Hamilton Fish settled in as secretary of state.

FIRST FAMILY

Of course, the new president had some ideas about what he wanted in the White House. First off, he wanted the first lady to be with him. Julia took measurements for new curtains and furniture right away, but she didn't move into the White House on inauguration day. Instead, she stayed in the Grants' I Street home, which she loved. Ulysses had to threaten to sell their home without her permission to get her to move. Two weeks after Grant became president, the first lady joined her husband at 1600 Pennsylvania Avenue. Daughter Nellie and eleven-year-old son Jesse lived in the executive mansion as well. Julia started a White House play group for her youngest son. He and his friends held their secret club meetings in a gardener's toolshed. Eighteen-year-old Fred was at West Point, and sixteen-year-old Ulysses Jr., whom the family called Buck, was starting at Harvard

Jesse, Julia, and Nellie

University. Nellie and Jesse went to school in Washington, D.C., riding to class in a yellow wicker pony cart.

The president continued to indulge his love of horses. He had new stables built at the White House. He once said that he would have liked the presidency more if Washington had better roads on which to race horses. One night when President Grant was out driving his carriage, a police officer who didn't recognize him stopped him and gave him a ticket for speeding. Grant praised the officer for doing his job.

Ulysses Grant did his best to fulfill his duties as president. Each morning he would read and write telegrams and letters until 10 A.M. Then he would meet with other government officials until noon. After lunch, he continued official business until 3 P.M. He liked to take walks each day, and on Sundays he would often walk six miles around Washington.

BOLSTERING THE GREENBACKS

The United States faced important economic decisions. The value of dollars, or greenbacks as they were called, had fallen during the Civil War. Four years of war had left a heavy national debt. President Grant knew it was essential that people in the United States and around the world trust the power of the dollar. "The first thing it seems to me is to establish the credit of the country. This is policy enough for the present," Grant said.

President Grant signed his first bill, the Act to Strengthen Public Credit, on March 18, 1869. This law guaranteed that people who held government bonds (promises to pay back money lent to the government during the Civil War) would get paid in gold or its equivalent.

The United States also had to settle a dispute with Great Britain that stemmed from the Civil War. British shipyards had built three cruisers, the *Alabama, Florida,* and *Shenandoah,* which the Confederates had used to attack Union ships. President Johnson and then President Grant wanted Britain to pay for the damages these ships had caused. Some people feared the matter would lead to another war between Britain and the United States. Grant understood that war was the last thing the nation needed.

He directed Secretary of State Hamilton Fish to negotiate a settlement. The agreement, called the Treaty of Washington, became a landmark of international relations when it went into effect on May 8, 1871. The treaty marked the first time countries agreed to abide by the decision of an arbitrator, an

Two Confederate ships built in Britain, the Florida *(top left) and the* Alabama *(bottom right) captured and looted more than one hundred ships that were attempting or thought to be attempting to deliver goods to the North.*

official not connected to either side, rather than going to war to settle their dispute. In the end, Britain agreed to apologize and to pay the United States $15.5 million.

BLACK FRIDAY

On September 24, 1869, the country came close to economic disaster. Two greedy investors named Jay Gould and Jim Fisk tried to corner the gold market. They wanted to buy up as much gold as possible so they could control the price of the precious metal. Gold was an essential part of the country's economy. Banks used the price of gold as a yardstick to determine the value of the dollar. As the price of gold rose, the value of the dollar dropped.

✧ ————————

In this cartoon, investor Jim Fisk is portrayed as the corrupt leader of a pack of dogs (thieves).

Gould and Fisk convinced Grant's brother-in-law, Abel Rathbone Corbin, to unwittingly become part of their scheme. Corbin, his wife, Virginia, and even the president's wife, Julia, all wanted to get in on the gold-buying fever. The Corbins did buy gold, but it's not clear whether Julia did. The president was unaware of the impending crisis.

Once Gould and Fisk's buying binge drove the price of gold from $135 an ounce to $161, Grant reacted quickly. He ordered Treasury Secretary George Boutwell to begin selling the government's own shares of gold. The extra gold available to the public caused the price to drop and ended the two investors' golden monopoly. Grant's actions marked the first time the U.S. government stepped in to control the economy.

RECONSTRUCTION

In 1870, during Reconstruction (the postwar period of rebuilding the South), the U.S. Congress passed the Fifteenth Amendment, giving black men the right to vote. In December of that year, Senator Hiram Revels of Mississippi and Representative Joseph Rainey of South Carolina became the first African American men to serve in Congress.

President Grant pushed former Confederate states to make sure their state governments upheld these new rights for African Americans. He wanted to make sure these states observed all the laws of the United States, not just those that benefited whites.

But throughout the country, many whites still considered blacks less than equal to whites. Many Southern whites were angry that African Americans were gaining rights and that

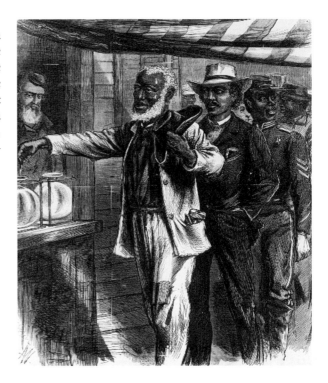

The Fifteenth Amendment to the Constitution gave black men the right to vote. It was ratified on February 3, 1870.

──────── ✧

the old Confederate way of life was disappearing. They joined the Ku Klux Klan and other secret societies, which terrorized and killed many black people. Grant was appalled. He signed the Ku Klux Klan Act in 1871 to give the U.S. government the power to act. Federal agents arrested more than five hundred suspected Klansmen.

Yet some members of Grant's family did not share his sense of fairness. At West Point, the president's son Fred had tried to force out James Webster Smith, the school's first African American cadet. Fred wrote that no "[black person] will ever graduate from West Point." Smith was court-martialed (put on trial by the armed forces) for marching with his head down. President Grant wrote to his war secretary, "Fred… informs me that the cadet [Smith] is very objectionable there." Fred was soon to graduate from West Point. Not wanting to "spoil the Grant family graduation celebration," the war secretary decided not to hear Smith's appeal of the court martial. The president attended Fred's graduation in 1871. Fred ranked last in discipline in his class of forty-one cadets.

A GROWING COUNTRY

Despite its economic pains, the country was growing. In less than ten years, the number of miles of railroad track in the United States almost doubled. Trains carried adventurers, settlers, farmers, and gold prospectors west. Settlers on the Great Plains were taking land that Native Americans had lived on for generations.

After Central Pacific railroad tracks (from the east) and Union Pacific tracks (from the west) met in Utah, the first North American transcontinental railroad opened the West to even more settlers.

Great White Father

During Grant's presidency, many whites considered Native Americans to be inferior in culture to people of European descent. But Grant believed Native Americans deserved equal treatment and the right to be American citizens. In 1870 the Fifteenth Amendment had given African Americans, but not Native Americans, the right to vote. (Native Americans didn't get the right to vote until 1924.) Grant blamed white settlers, not Native Americans, for the tensions between the two races. While stationed on the West Coast before the Civil War, Grant had written to Julia, "It really is my opinion that the whole race [Native Americans] would be harmless and peaceable if they were not put upon by whites." As president, Grant offered peace instead of war to Native American groups.

He tried to clean up the Bureau of Indian Affairs (BIA), the government agency established in 1824 to work with Native

Grant presented this medal (shown front and back)
to Nez Percé chief Joseph in 1871.

American nations. Many of the whites who worked as BIA agents cheated Native Americans out of the money and supplies they were due. In fact, Native Americans received only one-quarter of the funds that they were due by various treaty arrangements. "Our dealings with the Indian properly

Ely Parker
————— ✧ —————

lay us open to charges of cruelty and swindling," Grant said. To reduce corruption, Grant began appointing religious people, particularly Quakers, who had a reputation as peace-loving and honest, as Indian agents.

Grant named his former military secretary, a Native American named Ely Parker, to be commissioner of Indian affairs. This appointment was the highest rank a Native American had ever received in government. But after two years, Parker was forced to resign because of controversy about how he spent government money.

To reduce the risk of conflict between white settlers and Native Americans, Grant wanted to move Native Americans to reservations, land reserved only for them. Several Native American chiefs who wanted to move their tribes onto reservations went to Washington, D.C., to meet with Grant. He, like the Native American chiefs, had won his role as leader through war. The chiefs respected that, and they called Grant "Great White Father." The president did what he could to help Native Americans.

The Union Pacific Railroad hired Chinese laborers to lay new tracks east from California. They did most of the dangerous work with explosives and the dirty jobs no one else would do.

⸻ ✧ ⸻

In California, tensions were rising against the Chinese immigrants who had helped to build the railroads. In 1871 nineteen people died in an anti-Chinese riot in Los Angeles. Some Americans feared Chinese immigrants were taking too many American jobs. Grant did little to protect the immigrants, and eventually, Congress passed laws limiting how many Chinese could come to America.

Grant established the Justice Department to see that courts were properly run. He also created the Civil Service Commission, to try to make sure that government jobs were handed out to people of ability. The Civil Service Commission required that job seekers pass tests before being hired or promoted to many government jobs. The commission also protected government workers from losing their jobs when a new administration took office. A number of members of Congress resisted Grant's civil service reforms. They wanted to be able to hand out government jobs to their political friends.

ALL IN THE FAMILY

No president has given as many jobs to family members as Ulysses Grant did. The president named his son Buck as his private aide. Orvil Grant used his brother's famous name to make shady business deals and was also involved in a Native American trading-post scandal.

Julia's family benefited greatly from her husband's position, too. Her brother Fred became the president's secretary. Her brother John also received a share in an Indian trading post and ended up taking illegal profits from it. Julia's sister's husband became tax collector of the port of New Orleans and was caught up in a major scandal. Another Dent brother-in-law became Washington, D.C.'s marshal. Julia's sister, Nellie, filled in as White House hostess when the first lady was busy. Julia's father, Fred, lived in the White House until his death. His funeral was held in the White House Blue Room. In 1872 the *National Quarterly Review* called the Dent family the nation's worst criminal mob because they had received so many government jobs. One critic nicknamed the White House "the Dent family retreat."

————————————— ◇

This cartoon criticizes Grant for giving government jobs to family members (represented by the hats and footwear on the floor).

In 1872 President Grant named Yellowstone the first national park. At a time when railroad barons, ranchers, and settlers were carving up the West, Grant helped preserve precious property that Americans still enjoy.

✧ ———————————

Photographers on a special expedition to Yellowstone in 1871 photographed its many wonders, such as Old Faithful Geyser. When they later showed their work in Washington, D.C., their photos excited a lot of interest. Creating Yellowstone National Park was one of Grant's most farsighted acts as president.

CHAPTER SEVEN

LOYAL AND NAIVE BOSS

"Let no guilty man escape."
—Ulysses S. Grant, to the prosecutors on a court
case against one of his associates

Grant ran for reelection in 1872. But in September 1872, news broke that Vice President Schuyler Colfax had received shares of Union Pacific Railroad stock when he was Speaker of the House of Representatives. The railroad stock was thought to have been a bribe to keep Colfax and other members of Congress from investigating the railroad's illegal financial schemes. Republicans refused to allow Colfax to run for reelection with Grant. The Credit Mobilier bribery scandal, as the Union Pacific deal was called, ruined Colfax, but President Grant's reputation remained clean.

Grant's new vice presidential running mate was a former shoemaker, Senator Henry Wilson of Massachusetts. Wilson had also received some of the Union Pacific railroad stock,

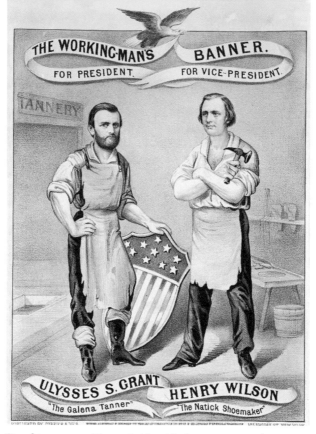

On this poster, Grant is identified as a tanner (someone who converts animal hides into leather) from Galena, Illinois, and Wilson as the shoemaker from Natick, Massachusetts.

———————— ◇ ————————

but the voters did not seem to mind and carried Grant and Wilson to victory.

The election of 1872 was the first in which large numbers of African American men had the chance to vote. No women of any race could cast ballots. Women's rights leader Susan B. Anthony was arrested on election day for attempting to vote. But the 1872 election also marked the first time a woman, a New York editor and social activist named Victoria Woodhull, ran for president.

Grant never promoted the rights of women, but during his administration, Anthony and other suffragettes (people

Susan B. Anthony
──────────── ✧

who fought for
women's suffrage—
the right to vote)
were organizing for equality. More than one hundred
women from seventeen states formed the Women's Christian
Temperance Union to promote women's rights and the
prohibition of alcohol.

Time and again, Grant sent federal troops to protect
black Americans in the South. Southern whites continued to
punish black independence and to seek to maintain racial
dominance by lashing out at African Americans. One of the
worst incidents occurred on Easter Sunday 1873 in Colfax,
Louisiana, in a county named Grant in honor of the war
hero. It was in Colfax that a mob of whites massacred more
than one hundred black people, many of whom were killed
after they had surrendered.

Eventually, the president realized the country—North
and South—was no longer willing to support a military
solution to every racial incident. Many, particularly white
Northerners, were growing tired of paying for troops to protect Southern blacks. They wanted the racial problems just
to go away. So Grant stopped sending troops to Southern

states. Blacks there were at the mercy of the white hate groups. Later, the Supreme Court overturned the convictions of the only three whites found guilty of the Colfax killings.

PANIC, DEPRESSION, AND STEADINESS

As President Grant began his second term, war debts continued to hamper the economy. September 1873 saw the collapse of many Wall Street businesses, including the country's most important and solid brokerage firm owned by financier Jay Cooke. The New York Stock Exchange closed for ten days. Wall Street's collapse led to a panic that sparked five years of economic depression. All around the country, people struggled to avoid bankruptcy. Factories and farms failed. Construction and new business stopped. During those years, Grant stayed true to his goal of reducing the national debt and stabilizing the country's money supply.

The biggest problem facing the country was inflation. The price of goods and services had risen so much that people didn't have enough money to buy what they needed. Many wanted the government to release more money—literally to print more dollar bills and put them into circulation—so people would have more money.

In 1874 Grant vetoed an inflation bill that would have increased the money supply. "I was never so pressed in my life to do anything as sign that bill—never," Grant wrote later. Republicans pleaded with Grant to sign the bill, saying their party would die unless the government released $100 million in greenbacks to ease the country's depression. But Grant stood firm. He believed more printed money would cause more inflation and instability. Grant's steadiness calmed a jittery country. Even his critics, such as wealthy New York lawyer George Templetom Strong, praised him. "This veto will rank in his record with Vicksburg and Appomattox," wrote Strong. The president's course of action helped the United States weather the economic depression and strengthened the value of the dollar. Grant considered his inflation bill veto to be one of his most important achievements as president.

A GILDED AGE WEDDING

In May 1874, the Grants' only daughter, Nellie, was married in an elaborate ceremony at the White House. Two hundred guests watched the spectacle, which featured eight bridesmaids, lavish garlands of white camellias, and a banquet featuring a fancy cake concocted by a White House chef. Ulysses Grant spent most of the wedding ceremony looking down at the floor, crying. Nellie was his favorite child. She was marrying a British man, Algernon Sartoris.

————————— ✧
Nellie and Algernon Sartoris

The young couple would soon leave for England to live there. Grant was deeply saddened by the thought of being separated from his only daughter.

The president was downcast, but Washington society felt uplifted. Nellie's wedding was the event of the season. It was the perfect opportunity to show off fancy clothes

———————————— ✧ ————————————

Nellie and Algernon got married in the East Room of the White House.

and give wildly expensive gifts. The wedding was a fitting symbol of the times, which author Mark Twain named the Gilded Age. Although most of the population worried about how to pay bills, the Civil War had produced many self-made millionaires—men who had been born in modest circumstances but had made fortunes during the war or in the boom afterward. The newly rich wanted to show off their wealth in extravagant fashions and ornately decorated homes.

Julia reveled in the chance to show off her daughter and the White House. The first lady loved entertaining in the nation's mansion. She held weekly receptions open to all. One social observer noted, "There were ladies from Paris in elegant attire and ladies from the interior [Midwest] in calico . . . ladies in diamonds, and others in dollar jewelry; chambermaids elbowed countesses, and all enjoyed themselves."

Julia and Ulysses both looked up to the successful captains of industry, the tycoons and millionaires who visited the White House. The Grants had received gifts—their homes in Galena, Philadelphia, and on I Street in Washington, D. C.—from rich friends who admired the general. Grant didn't seem to wonder why these wealthy patrons offered generous tributes. He was loyal and trustworthy and honest. Grant assumed others were the same way. He trusted the people around him. Grant's secretary of state, Hamilton Fish, once said, "I do not think it would have been possible for Grant to have told a lie, even if he had composed it and written it down." Unfortunately, many of the people around President Grant were far less honest than he was.

*Even Grant's private secretary, General Orville Babcock,
was put on trial in a bribery scandal.*

◇

SCANDALS

In June 1874, Treasury Secretary William Richardson was forced to resign after newspapers revealed that he had made a deal with a federal tax collector. The tax collector had agreed to keep half of the tax money he took in and split it with Richardson. In 1875 more corruption rocked the White House. The Whiskey Ring scandal involved midwestern liquor distillers who bribed federal officials to avoid paying millions of dollars in taxes. Eventually, more than three hundred people were caught in the bribery ring. The new treasury secretary, Benjamin Bristow, wanted trials to punish the offenders. Grant told prosecutors, "Let no guilty man escape."

But the president tried to protect one man who was implicated in the scandal. General Orville Babcock, the president's private secretary, was accused of being part of the conspiracy and was put on trial. After looking at the evidence, Grant was convinced his aide was innocent. He offered to testify on Babcock's behalf. Instead of giving testimony in court, Grant gave a five-hour deposition (out-of-court testimony), during which he answered lawyers' questions about Babcock and the scandal. It was the first time a sitting president gave a deposition in a criminal trial. Thanks to his loyal boss's support, Babcock was acquitted. In the end, about half of those who were charged in the Whiskey Ring Scandal pleaded guilty. A dozen fled the country, and only a few were convicted. But the guilty included another government official, the chief clerk of the U.S. Treasury.

One week after Babcock's trial ended, another White House official was in trouble. Secretary of War William Belknap and his wife, Carrie, were accused of extorting money from officials at military trading posts. Belknap gave

In this cartoon, Uncle Sam dives head first into a barrel of government scandals. The Belknaps' scheme to profit from military trading posts was just one of them.

someone the right to run the trading post at an army fort, and that person would then pay the Belknaps a share of the profits from the post's sales. Belknap quickly resigned.

The president didn't seem to understand the corruption around him. Senator James Garfield, who watched the unflappable president, wrote in his diary, "His imperturbability [calm] is amazing. I am in doubt whether to call it greatness or stupidity."

Political cartoons showed a president bent over with the weight of corrupt underlings. No one believed Ulysses Grant himself was dishonest, but the country was troubled by the continuing scandals that disrupted his presidency. Grant's mother, Hannah, did her best to defend the president, saying, "Every one of the people Ulysses has appointed were highly recommended to him by people who ought to know better."

Grant's mother, Hannah
——————— ✧ ———————

A HAPPY COUPLE

Throughout the scandals, Julia was the rock that kept Ulysses centered. The couple, both strong-willed, seemed tremendously well suited for one another. After years of marriage, they were as content as when they first fell in love. On May 22, 1875, the first lady wrote her husband a note, "How many days ago today is [it] that we were engaged: Just such a day as this too was it not?" He quickly wrote back, "Thirty-one years. I was so frightened however that I do not remember whether it was warm or snowing."

The Grants always liked to celebrate the anniversary of their engagement, rather than their actual wedding anniversary. Their long-distance engagement may have prepared them for the lengthy periods they spent apart during their marriage. The eight years in the White House would be the longest they had lived together in one place. Little wonder, then, that Julia loved being first lady. After years of being separated from her husband by economic hardship and war, she enjoyed the simple pleasure of being able to live together.

Julia never hesitated to give her husband advice. Sometimes Grant listened to his wife, other times he didn't. But the president knew it was hard to ignore Julia if she had a strong opinion. So when it came time to decide whether to run for a third term, Grant didn't consult with Julia. He made

✧ ——————
Julia enjoyed being first lady.

Grant is a trapeze artist in this cartoon. The scandals and corrupt associates of his presidency dangle from his teeth, as he contemplates "swinging" a third term.

---

the decision alone. Then he called a meeting of his cabinet, told them he had decided not to run again, and calmly walked to the post office to mail a letter to the Republican State Convention announcing his decision. When he returned, Julia said she knew something was going on and wanted to know what it was. Smiling, Grant told his wife he had decided not to seek a third term. Julia was heartbroken. She wrote later that she felt "deeply injured" her husband had made his decision without talking with her. She called their White House years "the happiest days of my life."

HANDLING ONE LAST PROBLEM

The presidential election of 1876 was greatly disputed. Neither Republican candidate Rutherford B. Hayes nor Democratic candidate Samuel Tilden received enough votes to win. No one was sure who had won the presidential vote in Florida, Louisiana, Oregon, or South Carolina. Both sides accused the other of election fraud. For a time, the country did not know who would follow Ulysses Grant in the White House. Eventually, Hayes was declared the winner, but controversy remained.

Grant's term was set to end on Sunday, March 4, 1877, and Hayes's inauguration was set for Monday, March 5. Because the election had been so disputed, Grant worried something might happen before Hayes took the oath of office. So on Saturday, March 3, the Grants had a large reception for the incoming president. As Julia Grant and Lucy Hayes entertained guests in the dining room, Ulysses Grant quietly steered Rutherford Hayes to the White House Red Room. There, Chief Justice Morrison Waite administered the oath of office to Hayes. Helping Rutherford B. Hayes become president two days early was Ulysses Grant's last official act as president.

At Grant's insistence, Rutherford B. Hayes took the oath of office two days before his public inauguration (above) outside of the Senate wing of the U.S. Capitol.

Grant enjoyed his time as president, but he acknowledged the corruption that would forever mark his administration. In his final address to Congress, Grant said, "It was my fortune, or misfortune, to be called to the office of the Chief Executive, without any previous political training. . . . Under such circumstances it is but reasonable to suppose that errors of judgment must have occurred. . . . Failures have been errors of judgment, not of intent." Those errors of judgment cast a shadow on Grant's presidency. The great general would not be remembered as a great president. Still, Grant had survived two full terms in office. He was the first president in thirty-one years to do so. Ten presidents before Grant had either not been reelected to office or had died during their second term.

Julia cried when it was time to leave their presidential home, saying, "Oh Ulys, I feel like a waif, like a waif on the world's wide common." For his part, Ulysses S. Grant was ready to step away from the heavy responsibilities of being president. He said he had never felt happier than the day he left the White House. "I felt like a boy getting out of school."

CHAPTER EIGHT

TRAVELER AND AUTHOR

"I believe myself that the [Civil War] was
worth all it cost us, fearful as that was. Since
it was over, I have visited every state in Europe
and a number in the East. I know as I did
not before the value of our inheritance."
—Ulysses S. Grant

When Hannah Simpson Grant chose Ulysses for her
son's middle name, she probably could not have imag-
ined he later would be known as a great world traveler,
like his namesake in Greek legends. Ever since he was a
child, Ulysses Grant loved to travel and see new places.
After he and Julia left the White House, they decided to
tour the world. The couple spent two and a half years
circling the globe with their teenaged son, Jesse.
Everywhere the Grants went, they were treated royally.

Although Grant was a former president, people around
the world called him General Grant. Even Julia's memoirs

refer to her husband as the General. To the many thousands of people who gathered to cheer Grant on his world tour, his military achievements were what mattered most. He was the most famous soldier in the world.

When crowds of British workers cheered Grant, they also called him the Emancipator (the freer of slaves). The world knew the American Civil War as a war to free slaves, and the world knew Ulysses S. Grant as the man who won the Civil War. The *London Times* noted that "after WASHINGTON, General GRANT is the president who will occupy the largest place in the history of the United States."

The Grants dined with Queen Victoria of England, greeted Belgian king Leopold, had an audience with the pope, and talked with Prince Bismarck of Germany. Grant and the German prince discussed military matters, but the great Civil War general told the famous German strategist, "I am more of a farmer than a soldier." In Japan Grant was the first person to have the privilege to shake the hand of the emperor, who was considered a god. In China General Li Hung-chang, the country's most powerful military leader, was quoted as saying, "You and I, General Grant, are the greatest men in the world."

The Grants savored the chance to see the world's wonders. One night the Greeks lit the Parthenon, an ancient temple in Athens, for the famous Americans. Grant and his wife saw the canals of Venice, the Ganges River of India, the pyramids of Egypt, and the gates of Jerusalem. Their thirty-month travels were paid for by Ulysses Grant's one good investment. Years earlier, Grant had bought shares in a mining operation that hit a rich vein of silver. When the money ran out, the Grants came home to the United States.

The Grants (front
row, seated second
and third from left)
*at the Temple of
Amon-Ra at
Karnak, Egypt*
──────────── ✧

In 1880 Grant's name came up again as a possible
Republican candidate for president. He received 304 votes on
the first ballot at the Republican Convention, short of the
379 votes needed for victory. Grant refused to go to the convention to ask for the nomination. Although by this time,
he wanted the job, he told Julia, "I would rather cut off my
right arm" than ask for it. That had always been Grant's
attitude—he didn't believe people should step forward to
promote themselves. "It is men who wait to be selected, and
not those who seek, from whom we may always expect
the most efficient service," he wrote in his memoirs. Grant's

decision to wait to be selected may have cost him his chance for a third term. In the end, the Republicans chose James A. Garfield as their candidate. Ulysses Grant needed to get a job to support his family. At that time, presidents didn't receive a pension—retirement income—and after all their travels, the Grants had little money left.

Buck Grant
——————— ✧ ———————

GRANT & WARD
Grant and his son Buck, a lawyer, went into business with a financial rising star, Ferdinand Ward. Ward was known as "the young Napoleon [emperor] of Wall Street." Their investment firm was called Grant & Ward. The Grant in the title actually referred to Buck, but most people assumed the general was the man behind the business.

But it was Ferdinand Ward who ran the firm. He saw to it that Grant & Ward made tremendous profits from 1881 to 1884. Ulysses Grant signed papers he didn't bother to read. He was making money and considered himself a millionaire. He wasn't paying attention to how the company was making that money.

On May 6, 1884, Grant went to the office, happy as usual. Then Buck Grant told his father, "Grant & Ward has failed, and Ward has fled." Ferdinand Ward had cheated the Grants and all their investors. Ulysses Grant stood in shock. All his money and that of most of his relatives had been tied up in the company. It was all gone. He was sixty-two years old and as destitute as when he and Julia had been struggling on their Hardscrabble farm. He told the company's cashier, "I have made it a rule of life to trust a man long after other people gave him up. I don't see how I can trust any human being again."

Ulysses and Julia had just $210. But when news spread about Grant & Ward's collapse and the general's bankruptcy, Grant's admirers, including railroad baron William Vanderbilt, came to the rescue. They sent checks and offered loans. Showman P. T. Barnum offered Grant $100,000 to display his Civil War memorabilia. Grant refused. Instead, most of Grant's military possessions—uniforms, swords, and trophies—were given in a trust to the government. They ended up at West Point and the Smithsonian Institution, a national museum.

Grant didn't want to profit from his role in the war. But he was still pressed for money. When a magazine editor asked him to write about key Civil War battles, Grant said yes. For $500 apiece, Grant wrote about Shiloh and Vicksburg. He wrote for four hours a day, seven days a week. He wrote despite feeling sick and weak. Soon he learned that he had throat cancer.

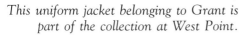

This uniform jacket belonging to Grant is part of the collection at West Point.

When his articles appeared in *Century* magazine, subscriptions rose dramatically. The editors asked Grant to write a book to be published by *Century* without any guarantee he would earn money from it.

When Grant's friend writer Mark Twain heard about the deal, he was stunned. He convinced Grant that he deserved better. Twain offered to publish Grant's memoirs himself and said Grant could take a generous cut of the profits.

Grant settled down to write his story. His throat cancer made eating and drinking painful, but he pressed on, writing for hours each day. The general who had refused to admit defeat at Fort Donelson and Shiloh and Vicksburg refused to yield to cancer. He continued to write as his health gave out. Grant was determined to finish his memoirs so that his family would have a source of income after his death. In March 1885, after much wrangling, Congress restored Ulysses Grant's rank and salary as General of the Army (a title he had given up when he became president). Even though he was retired, he would again receive a full military salary.

A page from one of Grant's articles that was published in Century *magazine*

✧

PERSONAL MEMOIRS OF U. S. GRANT.*

CHATTANOOGA.

AFTER the fall of Vicksburg I urged strongly upon the Government the propriety of a movement against Mobile. General Rosecrans had been at Murfreesboro', Tennessee, with a large and well-equipped army from early in the year 1863, with Bragg confronting him, with a force quite equal to his own at first, considering it was on the defensive. But after the investment of Vicksburg, Bragg's army was largely depleted to strengthen Johnston, in Mississippi, who was being reinforced to raise the siege. I frequently wrote to General Halleck suggesting that Rosecrans should move against Bragg. By so doing he would either detain the latter's troops, or lay Chattanooga open to capture. General Halleck strongly approved the suggestion, and finally wrote me that he had repeatedly ordered Rosecrans to advance, but that the latter had constantly failed to comply with the order, and at last, after having held a council of war, replied, in effect, that it was a military maxim "not to fight two decisive battles at the same time." If true, the maxim was not applicable in this case. It would be bad to be defeated in two decisive battles fought the same day, but it would not be bad to win them. I, however, was fighting no battle, and the siege of Vicksburg had drawn from Rosecrans's front so many of the enemy that his chances of victory were much greater than they would be if he waited until the siege was over, when these troops could be returned. Rosecrans was ordered to move against the army that was detaching troops to raise the siege. Finally he did move on the 24th of June, but ten days afterward Vicksburg surrendered, and the troops sent from Bragg were free to return. It was at this time that I recommended to the general-in-chief the movement against Mobile. I knew the peril the Army of the Cumberland was in, being depleted continually not only by ordinary casualties, but also by having to detach troops to hold its constantly extending line over which to draw supplies, while the enemy in front was as constantly being strengthened. Mobile was important to the enemy, and, in the absence of a threatening force, was guarded by little else than artillery. If threatened by land and from the water at the same time, the prize would fall easily, or troops would have to be sent to its defense. Those troops would necessarily come from Bragg.

My judgment was overruled, however, and the troops under my command were dissipated over other parts of the country where it was thought they could render the most service. Four thousand were sent to Banks, at New Orleans; five thousand to Schofield, to use against Price, in Arkansas; the Ninth Corps back to East Tennessee; and finally, in August, the whole of the Thirteenth Corps to Banks. I also sent Ransom's brigade to Natchez, to occupy that point, and to relieve Banks from guarding any part of the river above what he had guarded before the fall of Port Hudson. Ransom captured a large amount of ammunition and about five thousand beef cattle that were crossing the river going east for the rebel armies.

At this time the country was full of deserters from Pemberton's army, and it was reported that many had also left Johnston. These avowed they would never go back to fight against us again. Many whose homes were west of the river went there, and others went North to remain until they could return with security.

Soon it was discovered in Washington that Rosecrans was in trouble and required assistance. The emergency was now too immediate to allow us to give this assistance by making an attack in the rear of Bragg upon Mobile. It was therefore necessary to reënforce directly, and troops were sent from every available point. On the 13th of September Halleck telegraphed me to send all available forces to Memphis, and thence east along the Memphis and Charleston railroad to coöperate with Rosecrans. This instruction was repeated two days later, but I did not get even the first until the 23d of the month. As fast as transports could be provided all the troops except a portion of the Seventeenth Corps were forwarded under Sherman, whose services up to this time demonstrated his superior fitness for a separate command. I also moved McPherson, with most of the troops still about Vicksburg, eastward, to compel the enemy to keep back a force to meet him. Meanwhile Rosecrans had very skillfully manœuvred Bragg south of the Tennessee River, and through and beyond Chattanooga. If he had stopped and intrenched, and made himself strong there, all would have been right, and the mistake of not moving earlier partially compensated. But he pushed on, with his forces very much scattered, until Bragg's

*Copyright, 1885, by U. S. Grant. All rights reserved.

Although he was growing weaker, Grant persevered. The last famous photograph of Ulysses Grant shows a gaunt bearded man, wrapped in blankets, a stocking cap covering his head and a blanket shielding one side of his face, sitting calmly in a wicker chair on a porch. He isn't looking at the camera. Grant is focused on the notebook in his hand as he writes. Long after he was too weak to sit at a desk, he sat in a chair, gripping a pencil as he finished his memoirs. His family brought him to a summer cottage in Mount McGregor, New York. It was there that longtime friends and military men from the North and the South came to say good-bye. Cancer made speaking impossible, so Grant wrote notes on a small pad of paper. He used the pad to converse with one of his last visitors, former Confederate general Simon Bolivar Buckner. The two men had been friends at

─────────────── ✧
*Grant continued writing
in spite of his illness.*

West Point and during the Mexican War, then enemies in the Civil War, where Grant demanded Buckner's unconditional surrender at Fort Donelson, then friends again. Grant wrote Buckner, "I have witnessed since my sickness just what I wished to see ever since the war: harmony and good feeling between the sections [North and South]."

Grant seemed to have found peace and harmony in his last year. He set down his pencil on July 16, saying his memoirs were complete. In his last note to his doctor, the sixty-three-year-old general wrote, "There never was one more willing to go than I am." On the morning of July 23, 1885, one week after finishing his book, Ulysses S. Grant died quietly in his sleep.

Grant's family requested a military funeral in New York City. Grant had wanted both Northern and Southern generals as pallbearers. His friends William Tecumseh Sherman and Philip Sheridan of the Union and Joseph E. Johnston and Simon Bolivar Buckner of the Confederacy carried the casket. More than one million people lined the funeral route. Veterans of the Confederate Stonewall Brigade marched alongside veterans from the North's Grand Army of the Republic. Not since the assassination of Abraham Lincoln had so many Americans turned out to mark one man's death.

The sixty thousand mourners in the parade walked slowly to New York City's Riverside Park, where Grant was buried on a bluff overlooking the Hudson River. Grant's Tomb, a white marble dome with imposing bronze doors, faces south, toward Appomattox. Emblazoned on the monument are the general's famous words, "Let us have peace."

Ulysses Grant died knowing that the country he had fought for was at peace. And he died having finished memoirs

Grant's funeral procession in New York reminded people of Lincoln's funeral.

— ◇ —

that would make history. He was the first U.S. president to publish a book. Grant's memoirs, titled *The Personal Memoirs of U.S Grant,* sold more than 300,000 copies, and it is still considered one of the finest books on American military history. Two years after publication, Mark Twain presented Julia with a check for $200,000. Eventually Grant's book would bring his family more than $450,000. The memoirs were written in a simple and straightforward manner, much like Grant himself. Near the end of the book, Grant wrote, "I feel that we are on the eve of a new era, when there is to be great harmony between the Federal [Northerner] and Confederate. I cannot stay to be a living witness to the correctness of this prophecy; but I feel it within me that it is to be so."

TIMELINE

1822   Ulysses Grant is born in Point Pleasant, Ohio, on April 27.

1843   Grant graduates from West Point. He meets Julia Dent.

1844   Julia and Ulysses become secretly engaged in May.

1846   Lieutenant Grant serves in the Mexican War.

1848   Ulysses and Julia marry on August 22.

1850   Frederick Dent Grant is born.

1852   Grant goes to California with the U.S. Fourth Infantry. His son Ulysses (Buck) Simpson Grant is born.

1854   Grant is relieved of military duty. He returns to St. Louis, Missouri, as a civilian.

1855   Ellen (Nellie) Wrenshall Grant is born.

1860   After farm and business failures, Grant joins his father's leather goods business in Galena, Illinois.

1861   The Civil War begins. Grant becomes commander of the Twenty-first Illinois Volunteers.

1862   Brigadier General Grant seizes Fort Donelson, Tennessee, and demands unconditional surrender. Grant defeats Confederates at the bloody Battle of Shiloh.

1863   Grant wins Vicksburg seige on July 4.

1864   President Abraham Lincoln promotes Grant to Lieutenant General of the Army. Robert E. Lee defeats Grant at the Battle of the Wilderness and again at Cold Harbor, Virginia. Grant sets up headquarters at City Point, Virginia. Lincoln is reelected.

1865 Lee surrenders to Grant at Appomattox Court House, Virginia, on April 12. Lincoln is shot at Ford's Theatre and dies on the morning of April 15. Grant helps President Johnson with Lincoln's funeral and the start of Reconstruction.

1868 President Johnson is impeached. Grant is elected president.

1869 Black Friday occurs on Wall Street on September 24.

1872 The Union Pacific Railroad bribery scandal breaks. Grant is reelected president.

1873 In April a massacre in Colfax, Louisiana, leaves more than one hundred African Americans dead. In September Jay Cooke's brokerage firm collapses, and economic panic hits and begins five years of nationwide depression.

1874 President Grant vetoes an inflation bill. Nellie Grant is married at the White House.

1875 President Grant gives sworn testimony in the Whiskey Ring scandal trial.

1877 Grant and Julia begin a two-and-a-half-year world tour.

1880 Grant fails to win the Republican nomination for president.

1881 Grant goes into business with son Buck and Ferdinand Ward.

1884 Grant & Ward firm goes bankrupt in May. Grant begins writing Civil War articles and then his memoirs. Doctors determine that Grant has throat cancer.

1885 Grant finishes writing his memoirs, *The Personal Memoirs of U.S. Grant,* on July 16. Ulysses S. Grant dies peacefully on July 23. Grant's funeral draws 1.5 million mourners.

1887 Mark Twain presents Julia with a check of $200,000 for sales of Grant's memoirs. (More than 300,000 two-volume sets are sold. Julia eventually receives more than $420,000.)

SOURCE NOTES

7 *Civil War Times Illustrated* editors, *Great Battles of the Civil War* (New York: Gallery Books, 1984), 84.

8 James V. Murfin, *Battlefields of the Civil War* (New York: Portland House, 1990), 103.

8 Jean Edward Smith, *Grant* (New York: Simon & Schuster, 2001), 201.

8 Geoffrey C. Ward, *The Civil War: An Illustrated History* (New York: Alfred A. Knopf, 1991), 120.

8 Smith, 200.

9 Ward, 124.

10 Ulysses S. Grant, *Ulysses S. Grant: Memoirs and Selected Letters: Personal Memoirs of U.S. Grant/Selected Letters 1839–1865,* ed. Mary McFeeley and William S. McFeeley, (New York: Library of America, 1990), 31.

10–11 Ibid., 26.

11 Ibid., 22.

12 Ibid.

13 Ibid., 31.

13 Ibid., 29.

15 Ibid., 34.

16 Smith, 86.

17 Grant., 897.

17 Ibid., 65.

18 Ibid., 41.

19 Ibid., 70.

21 Smith, 82.

22 Grant, 938.

25 Smith, 91.

25 Ibid., 93.

26 Ibid., 92.

26 Ibid., 93.

28 Grant, 164.

29 Smith, 108.

30 Grant, 165.

30 Smith, 118.

31 Ibid., 158.

31 Grant, 208.

32 Ibid., 410.

32 Smith, 160.

32 Ibid.

32 Ibid., 348.

33 Ibid.

33 Ibid., 164.

33 Ibid., 166.

35 Ibid., 199.

35 F. Norton Boothe, *Great American Generals: Ulysses S. Grant* (New York: Brompton Books Corp., 1990), 23.

35 Grant, 238.

38 James M. McPherson, ed., *To the Best of My Ability: The American Presidents* (New York: Dorling Kindersley, 2000), 138.

38 Ward, 127.

39 Grant, 381.

39 Harvey M. Trimble, War Diary, 22 May 1863, 93rd Illinois, Regimental Files, Vicksburg National Military Park, Vicksburg, MS. Quoted in James R. Arnold and Roberta Wiener, *This Unhappy Country: The Turn of the Civil War, 1863* (Minneapolis: Lerner Publications Company, 2002), 32.

41 Smith, 404.

41 Grant, 390.

42 Smith, 285.

43 Ward, 276.

44 Grant, 469.

44 Ibid., 232.

44–45 Ibid., 475.

45 Ibid., 512.

46 Smith, caption to illustration #24, ch. 4

46 Ibid., 349.

47 Ward, 295.

47 Smith, 364.

48 Judith St. George, *So You Want to Be President?* (New York: Philomel Books, 2000), 28.
50 Paul F., Boller, *Presidential Wives: An Anecdotal History* (New York: Oxford University Press, 1988), 136.
50–51 Smith, 376.
52 Ibid., 399.
52 Ward, 377.
52 Ibid., 378.
53 Smith, 406.
53 Ibid., 409.
54 Brooks D. Simpson, *Let Us Have Peace: Ulysses S. Grant and the Politics of War and Reconstruction, 1861–1868* (Chapel Hill, NC: The University of North Carolina Press, 1991), 246.
56 Smith, 410.
56 Simpson, 91–92.
56 Smith, 410.
58 Ibid., 99.
58 Ibid.
62 Smith, 427.
62 Ibid.
63 Ibid., 451.
64 Ibid., 456.
64 Simpson, 246.
65 Ibid., 251.
67 Smith, 520.
67 Boothe, 69.
70 Smith, 481.
73 Carl Sferrazza Anthony, *America's First Families: An Inside View of Two Hundred Years of Private Life in the White House* (New York: Simon & Schuster, 2000), 187.
75 Ibid.,187.
75 Ibid.
76 Smith, 520.
77 Ibid., 523.
81 McPherson, 135.

84 Smith, 580.
85 Ibid.
87 Boller, 134.
87 Smith, 592.
88 McPherson, 135.
90 Smith, 595.
90 Anthony, 127.
91 Ibid., 196.
92 Juddi Morris, *At Home with the Presidents* (New York: John Wiley & Sons, 1999), 72.
94 Boothe, 72.
94 Boller, 138.
94 Smith, 605.
95 Ibid., 626.
96 William S. McFeely, *GRANT: A Biography* (New York: W. W. Norton & Company, 1982), 457.
96 McPherson, 134.
96 Boothe, 72.
97 Smith, 616.
97 Grant, 470.
98 Boothe, 73.
98 Smith, 671.
99 Richard Goldhurst, *Many Are the Hearts: The Agony and the Triumph of Ulysses S. Grant* (New York: Reader's Digest Press, 1975), 8.
102 Ibid., 225.
102 Ibid., 227.
103 Grant, 779.

SELECTED BIBLIOGRAPHY

Anthony, Carl Sferrazza. *America's First Families: An Inside View of Two Hundred Years of Private Life in the White House.* New York: Simon & Schuster, 2000.

Boller, Paul F., Jr. *Presidential Wives: An Anecdotal History.* New York: Oxford University Press, 1988.

Brinkley, Alan, and Davis Dyer, eds. *The Reader's Guide to the American Presidency.* New York: Houghton Mifflin Co., 2000.

Catton, Bruce. *U. S. Grant and the American Military Tradition.* New York: Grosset & Dunlap, 1954.

Civil War Times Illustrated editors. *Great Battles of the Civil War.* New York: Gallery Books, 1984.

Golay, Michael. *A Ruined Land: The End of the Civil War.* New York: John Wiley & Sons, 1999.

Goldhurst, Richard. *Many Are the Hearts: The Agony and Triumph of Ulysses S. Grant.* New York: Reader's Digest Press, 1975.

Grant, Ulysses S. *Memoirs and Selected Letters: Personal Memoirs of U. S. Grant/Selected Letters 1839–1865.* Edited by Mary McFeely and William S. McFeely. New York: Library of America, 1990.

McFeely, William S. *GRANT: A Biography.* New York: W. W. Norton & Company, 1982.

McPherson, James M., ed. *To the Best of My Ability: The American Presidents.* New York: Dorling Kindersley, 2000.

Morris, Juddi. *At Home with the Presidents.* New York: John Wiley & Sons, 1999.

Murfin, James V. *Battlefields of the Civil War.* New York: Portland House, 1990.

Simpson, Brooks D. *Let Us Have Peace: Ulysses S. Grant and the Politics of War and Reconstruction, 1861–1868.* Chapel Hill, NC: The University of North Carolina Press, 1991.

Smith, Carter, ed. *One Nation Again: A Sourcebook on the Civil War.* Brookfield, CT: The Millbrook Press, 1993.

Smith, Jean Edward. *Grant.* New York: Simon & Schuster, 2001.

Taylor, Tim. *The Book of Presidents.* New York: Arno Press, 1972.

Ward, Geoffrey C. *The Civil War: An Illustrated History.* New York: Alfred A. Knopf, 1991.

FOR FURTHER READING AND WEBSITES

Bausum, Ann. *Our Country's Presidents.* Washington, D.C.: National Geographic Society, 2001.

Biography of Ulysses S. Grant
<http://www.whitehouse.gov/history/presidents/ug18.html>

Blue, Rose, and Corrine J. Nader. *Who's That in the White House? The Expansion Years: 1857–1907.* Austin, TX: Raintree Steck-Vaughn, 1998.

Boothe, F. Norton. *Great American Generals: Ulysses S. Grant.* New York: Brompton Books Corp., 1990.

Damon, Duane. *Growing Up in the Civil War.* Minneapolis: Lerner Publications Company, 2003.

———. *When This Cruel War Is Over: The Civil War Home Front.* Minneapolis: Lerner Publications Company, 1996.

Day, Nancy. *Your Travel Guide to Civil War America.* Minneapolis: Runestone Press, 2001.

Marin, Albert. *Unconditional Surrender: U. S. Grant and the Civil War.* New York: Atheneum, 1994.

Roberts, Jeremy. *Abraham Lincoln.* Minneapolis: Lerner Publications Company, 2004.

Ulysses S. Grant
<http://www.americanpresidents.org/presidents/president.asp?PresidentNumber=18>
A brief biography of the president, other articles about his family and administration, and links.

INDEX

Act to Strengthen Public Credit, 70
African Americans, 56, 60–61, 73–75,
76, 82, 83–84
Appomattox Court House, 52, 54; treaty
at, 57, 59

Babcock, Orville, 88–89
battles, descriptions of, 7–9, 30–31, 35,
45, 47, 99
Belknap, William and Carrie, 89–90
Black Friday, 72–73
Boggs, Harry and Louise, 26
Bureau of Indian Affairs (BIA), 76–77

Chinese Americans, 78
civil rights, 60–61, 73–74, 76, 82–83
Civil Service Commission, 78
Civil War, 7–9, 66; beginning of, 27;
causes of, 19–20, 27; cost of, 55, 70,
95; deaths in, 8, 9, 35, 45, 46, 47; end
of, 52–53, 55; map of, 36–37
Civil War, battles and sieges of: Atlanta,
45, 51; Battle of the Wilderness,
45–46; Chattanooga, 42, 49; Cold
Harbor, 46–47; Fort Donelson, 30–33;
Fort Sumter, 27; Petersburg, 51;
Richmond, 45, 46, 47, 52, 53; Shiloh,
7–9, 34–35, 38, 99; Spotsylvania, 46;
Vicksburg, 38–39, 42, 99
Colfax, LA, massacre, 83–84
Colfax, Schuyler, 64, 81
Confederacy: anthem of, 54; borders of,
30; defeat of, 39; formation of, 27;
map of, 36–37; president of, 8, 38, 49;
vice president of, 60
Confederate army, 7–9, 29–31, 35, 38,
42, 51, 52–53; generals in: Beauregard,
8; Buckner, 22–23, 31, 33, 101–102;
Harris, 29; Johnston, A., 7, 8, 35;
Johnston, J., 45, 52, 57–58, 102; Lee,
45, 46, 47, 51–53, 54, 59; Longstreet,
25, 50

Davis, Jefferson, 8, 38, 49
debts, national, 70, 84
Dent, Fred (brother-in-law), 16, 24, 79
Dent, Fred (father-in-law), 17, 79

economics, 70, 72–73, 75, 76, 77, 83,
84–85, 87
election of 1876, 92

Fish, Hamilton, 68, 71, 87
Fort Humbolt, 22
Fort Vancouver, 21
Fourth Infantry, 16, 21

Galena, Illinois, 26, 27, 59, 65, 87
gold market, 72–73
Grant, Ellen (Nellie) Wrenshall
(daughter), 23, 59, 67, 85–87
Grant, Frederick Dent (son), 20, 21, 42,
59, 68, 74–75
Grant, Hannah (mother), 10, 12, 21, 24,
90, 95
Grant, Jesse (father), 10, 11, 12, 21,
23–24, 26
Grant, Jesse Root (son), 26, 50, 59, 68,
69, 95
Grant, Julia Dent (wife), 16–17, 20, 21,
23, 24, 26, 50, 56, 59, 65, 68–69, 73,
79, 87, 90–91, 92, 93, 94, 95–96, 99,
103
Grant, Ulysses (Buck) Simpson (son), 21,
59, 69, 79, 98
Grant, Ulysses S.: and alcohol, 22, 28,
34, 49; birth and childhood of,
10–12; candidate for presidency, 42,
64–65, 81–82, 91–92, 96; and cigars,
33, 49; death of, 102–103; as farmer,
23, 25–26, 96; health of, 15, 26, 41,
99, 100–101; and horses, 10–12, 15,
16, 18, 32, 40, 41, 49, 51, 69; letters
of, 17, 21, 22, 31, 33, 62, 63;
memoirs of, 44, 99–101, 102–103;

and money, 22, 23, 24, 26–27, 33, 59, 87, 96, 98–99, 103; names of, 10, 14, 17, 33, 95, 96; personality of, 8–9, 11, 21, 32, 43, 87, 90; as quartermaster, 17–18, 20, 21, 22; and racism, 60, 61, 62, 73–74, 76, 83–84; and slavery, 24; and West Point, 10, 12–15, 16, 25, 27, 28, 31, 32, 68, 74–75, 99, 102;
Grant & Ward, 98–99
Great Britain, 71–73

Halleck, Henry, 34
Hardscrabble farm, 23, 25–26
Hayes, Rutherford B., 93

Johnson, Andrew, 32, 56–57, 59, 60–61, 71; impeachment of, 63; tensions with Grant, 62–63
Jones, William, 24
Justice Department, 78

Ku Klux Klan (KKK), 60, 74

Lincoln, Abraham, 27, 30, 33, 38, 42, 43, 44, 50–51, 54–55, 73; assassination of, 56

map, 36–37
Mexican War, 16–19
Mississippi River, 38, 42, 44–45

Native Americans, 14, 76–77, 83
New York Independent, 63

Parker, Ely, 77

racism, 60–61, 62, 73–75, 76, 78, 83
railroads, 13, 75, 78, 80; scandals and, 81
Rainey, Joseph, 73
Rawlins, John, 49, 50, 68
Reconstruction, 73–74
Reid, Whitelaw, 8
Revels, Hiram, 73

rivers, 7, 30, 38, 44–45, 47

scandals and corruption, 72–73, 76–77, 79, 81, 88–91, 92
Seymour, Horatio, 65
slavery, 19, 23–24, 27, 57, 73
Smith, James Webster, 74–75
Stanton, Edwin, 43, 62–63
Stephens, Alexander, 60
Stevens, Thaddeus, 60
surrender, terms of, 31, 33, 52–53, 57–58

Taylor, Zachary, 19
Tenure of Office Act, 63
Texas, 16, 19
Treaty of Washington, 71
Twain, Mark, 87, 100, 103

Union army, 7–9, 30–31, 34–35, 38, 41, 42, 44, 46; generals in: Halleck, 34; McClellan, 22, 28–29; Sheridan, 46, 47, 55, 58, 102; Sherman, 9, 25, 35, 51, 55, 57–58, 102
Union navy, 30–31, 71
U.S. Army, 59, 83
U.S. Congress, 19, 63, 74, 78, 101

Ward, Ferdinand, 98
Washburne, Elihu, 29, 68
Washington, D.C., 42–43, 55, 58–59, 69
Washington, George, 33, 42, 48, 67
Watkins, Sam, 8
West Point, 10, 12–15, 16, 25, 27, 28, 31, 32, 68, 74–75, 99, 102
Whiskey Ring Scandal, 88–89
White House, 68, 69, 79, 86, 87
Wilson, Henry, 81–82
women, rights of, 82–83
Women's Christian Temperance Union, 83

Yellowstone National Park, 80

About the Author

Kate Havelin was in junior high when she decided to be a writer. She edited her high school and college newspapers and studied journalism. After graduating, she worked as a television producer for more than a decade. This is Havelin's tenth book for young readers. She lives with her husband and two sons in St. Paul, Minnesota.

❖

Photo Acknowledgments

Photographs in this book appear with the permission of: West Point Museum Collection, United States Military Academy, pp. 2, 44, 48, 99; National Archives, pp. 6, 29, 77; Library of Congress, pp. 9 (LC-USZ62-3581), 11 (LC-USZ62-23789), 13 (LC-USZC2-3141), 14 (LC-USZC2-1877), 19 (LC-USZ62-7559), 21 (LC-USZ61-496), 22 (HABS, CAL, 12-EUR, 5-1), 23 (LC-USZ62-110714), 24 (HABS, MO, 95-AFT.V, 1B-2), 25 (LC-USZ62-101486), 27 (LC-USZC4-528), 31 (LC-USZC4-1764), 34 (LC-B813- 6377A), 39 (LC-USZC2-499), 40 (LC-USZ62-101396); 43 (LC-USZ6-82), 46 (LC-B8171-2509), 47(LC-USZ62-131934), 50 (LC-B8171-3400), 51 (LC-USZ62-116520), 53 (LC-USZ62-132504), 55 (LC-USZ62-104551), 58 (LC-USZ62-99600), 61 (LC-USZ62-111070), 63 (LC-DIG-cwpb-06437), 66 (LC-USZ62-4912), 69 (LC-DIG-cwpbh-00519), 71 (top) (LC-USZ62-125982), (bottom) (LC-USZ62-14103), 72 (LC-USZ62-091512), 74 (LC-USZ62-97946), 75 (LC-USZ62-116354), 82 (LC-USZ62-3983), 83 (LC-USZ62-7140), 85 (LC-DIG-cwpbh-05134), 88 (LC-USZ62-101403), 90 (LC-USZ62-101878), 91 (LC-USZ62-34809), 92 (LC-USZCN4-322), 93 (LC-USA7-29858), 97 (LC-USZ62-092457), 98 (LC-USZ62-101866), 101 (LC-USZ62-7607), 103 (LC-USZC4-1814); Minnesota Historical Society, pp. 12, 18; © Minnesota Historical Society, pp. 12, 18; © CORBIS, p.17; © Hulton|Archive by Getty Images, p. 20; © Laura Westlund, pp. 36–37; © Medford Historical Society Collection/CORBIS, p. 49; © Argosy Bookstore, New York, p. 57; © Smithsonian Institution, p. 59; Minneapolis Public Library, p. 62; © David J. & Janice L. Frent Collection/CORBIS, p. 65; MSCUA, University of Washington Libraries, p.76 (left [NA955], right [NA954]); California Historical Society, San Francisco, p.78 [GS Social Groups: Chinese I: 25345]; © Bettmann/CORBIS, pp. 79, 89; Yellowstone National Park Collection, p. 80; New York Public Library, p. 86; Courtesy of Cornell University Library, Making of America Digital Collection, *The Century,* vol. 31, issue 1 (Nov. 1885), p. 100.

Cover: Library of Congress (LC-USZ62-13018 DLC)